KW-054-938

THE OPEN UNIVERSITY

Arts : A Third Level Course
Twentieth Century Poetry

Unit 1

ENGLISH POETRY IN 1912

Prepared by Graham Martin for the Course Team

The Open University Press

Quarto
821.9109

Cover design based on art nouveau typography of the early twentieth century

CHRIST'S COLLEGE
LIBRARY

Access on No. **57512**

Class No. Q.
821.9109.

Catal.

− 2/77

The Open University Press
Walton Hall Milton Keynes

First published 1975

Copyright © 1975 The Open University

All rights reserved. No part of this work may be reproduced in any form, by mimeograph or any other means, without permission in writing from the publisher.

Designed by the Media Development Group of the Open University.

Printed in Great Britain by
EYRE AND SPOTTISWOODE LIMITED
AT GROSVENOR PRESS PORTSMOUTH

ISBN 0 335 05100 6

This text forms part of an Open University course. The complete list of units in the course appears at the end of this text.

For general availability of supporting material referred to in this text please write to the Director of Marketing, The Open University, P.O. Box 81, Walton Hall, Milton Keynes, MK7 6AT.

Further information on Open University courses may be obtained from the Admissions Office, The Open University, P.O. Box 48, Walton Hall, Milton Keynes, MK7 6AB.

1.1

CONTENTS   UNIT 1

AIMS AND OBJECTIVES

Unit 1 has three principal aims

a   To outline the main reason for beginning the study of twentieth-century poetry in the year 1912.

b   To give you experience of reading poems carefully and formulating your own views about them.

.c   To discuss the poetry of the Georgian movement.

I have sometimes added to my own comments on poems under discussion, the differing opinions expressed by colleagues in the course team, both for their intrinsic interest, and to underline the all important lesson that there is no 'right response' to a poem.

I would particularly like to acknowledge the helpfulness of comments and criticisms of the first draft of the unit by Richard Allen, Alasdair Clayre, Roger Day, Nick Furbank, John Selwyn Gilbert, Mrs Cicely Havely, Miss Susan Khin Zaw, Ken Mackenzie, John Purkis, Mrs Prudence Smith and Keith Whitlock.

ENGLISH POETRY IN 1912

1 INTRODUCTION

1.1 'But why 1912?' you may well want to ask, and this is a fair question. Before answering it, though, let me first try to deal with the more general one lurking behind it. 'Why begin with a date at all? Dates mean chronology, and chronology means literary history, and while that has its place, the poetry should come first. Why not, then, begin with a poet?' When we planned this course, we discussed these issues repeatedly and at length. We considered a different structure altogether, which tried to side-step the question of chronology by concentrating on the work of half a dozen major poets for, say, five weeks apiece. Yet even in the case of a single poet, dates, chronology, kept coming up. Any poet writes his poems in chronological order. As often as not, his later work has developed from, has reacted against, his earlier. It is sometimes the mark of a great poet that, taken as a whole, his work reveals a unity altering one's feeling about the individual poems that make it up. So, to study even one major poet on his own means looking at the relationships between poems, as well as at the poems themselves, and these relationships involve some attention to chronology. Then again, to study only major poets can lead to a misleading notion about literature, as if it were a mountain range, all peaks and no foothills. Great poetry does not grow in isolation. It needs the stimulus of good poetry, the kind we call 'minor' and embalm in period anthologies, and maybe even a lot of bad poetry, happily forgotten. We get no sense of scale if we read only the major figures, and no sense of their creative power over those who follow them, and that, really, is the point of literary history. So, in one way or another, the study of even a single poet moves necessarily towards a process of comparison and contrast between poem and poem and then between poet and poet, and because poets write and publish at particular moments in time, that means at some point, chronology.

1.2 Those were the general reasons, applying to any body of poetry, or indeed of literature. But there was a particular reason as well. In literature and the arts, as in 'history', every now and again changes of quite exceptional energy and extent come about which seem to justify the use of some such term as 'revolution'. Such changes can only be described in a chronological and historical way. Twentieth-century poetry began in one of those striking changes of direction. Or, if that seems to beg too many questions, or to imply that suddenly all the poems written after 1900 were radically different from those written before, then we can say that certain energetic, talented and influential poets in the opening years of this century had 'revolutionary' aims. They were hostile to the influence of most nineteenth-century English poetry, and as is so often the way with 'revolutionaries' they were concerned not so much with rejecting the past as reshaping it, proposing 'new fathers' in place of the old Romantic and Victorian models.

1.3 Look at this short poem.

> *In a Station of the Metro*
> The apparition of these faces in the crowd;
> Petals on a wet, black bough.

What does it say? What is it about? Is it a description, and if so, to what point? Would we even think of it as a whole poem if it did not have a title? Or is it really a prose fragment set out on the page to look like a poem?

Perhaps, today, we ask these questions less insistently than we would if our only experience of poetry were based on this:

Song

April, April,
Laugh thy girlish laughter;
Then, the moment after,
Weep thy girlish tears!
April, thàt mine ears
Like a lover greetest,
If I tell thee, sweetest,
All my hopes and fears,
April, April,
Laugh thy golden laughter,
Weep thy golden tears!

It rhymes, it has a metrical scheme, it could never be mistaken for prose. It is *about* something. The weather? Love? Well, something . . . We feel sure about that, and we feel sure, too, that it is a *poem*. It was against that kind of unshakeable confidence about what was, and what was not a poem, that the twentieth-century revolution in poetry was aimed.

1.4   The second poem, written by William Watson (1858–1935), was first published in 1895, and not long afterwards it was chosen for inclusion in the *Oxford Book of English Verse* (1900). Clearly, it suited prevailing notions about poetry. The first poem, written by Ezra Pound (1885–1972), appeared in 1916. Pound was one of the authors of the 'new poetry', and a major influence on others. Indeed, the whole period has been called 'The Age of Pound' by Hugh Kenner, an outstanding scholar and critic of twentieth-century poetry. The difference between the two poems is the kind of thing T. S. Eliot (1888–1965) may have had in mind when he remarked, in an introduction to Pound's essays appearing in 1954, 'the situation of poetry in 1909 or 1910 was stagnant to a degree difficult for any young poet of today to imagine'. (*Literary Essays of Ezra Pound*, ed. Eliot, p xiii.) Since Eliot is the other major 'revolu-

Figure 1   Edward Thomas by J. Thomas, 1905
(National Portrait Gallery)

Figure 2   Robert Graves by J. Aldridge, 1968 (National Portrait Gallery)

tionist' of the period, we do not now necessarily have to accept that statement as gospel. Whether English poetry in 1909–10 really was stagnant, whether and in what ways the new kind of poetry written by Pound and Eliot was 'revolutionary', and whether, as an influence, it was altogether beneficial, are necessary questions, and will be discussed, some here, some in later units. At the moment, all I am proposing is that to come to terms with the mainstream of twentieth-century poetry, some history, some notion of dates and influences is an essential part of our study. 'Revolutions' take place in time, and even though what we are chiefly interested in is the 'new', part of its identity was created by the process of overcoming the 'old'.

1.5   Which brings me back to the question 'Why 1912?' Eliot speaks of 1909–10. Pound was an active force in London literary life from 1909, the date of his *Personae* and also, as it happens, of Eliot's first important poem, 'Portrait of a Lady', though Eliot himself was not resident in London till 1914. So, if we are looking for a single date for the beginnings of twentieth-century poetry, 1909 has a strong claim. We have picked 1912 because by that date another new poetic movement was under way, less high-powered and more 'native' than the one set going by Pound and Eliot. This movement is known as the Georgian movement, taking its name from George V, who came to the throne in 1910. The first collection of poems, *Georgian Poetry*, appeared in 1912. The Georgian poets were not as individual as Eliot or Pound, nor were they as single-minded in their thinking about poetry. But they were against similar things in the poetry of the immediate past, and their liberating impact on some readers may be judged by a comment of D. H. Lawrence (1885–1930) – who called the first Georgian anthology 'a big breath taken when we are waking up after a night of oppressive dreams'. (*D. H. Lawrence: Selected Literary Criticism*, ed. Beal, p 72.)

There was no one outstanding Georgian poet, but Edward Thomas (1878–1917), Wilfred Owen (1893–1918) and Robert Graves (b. 1895), had their roots in the movement, and it has been suggested that if Thomas and Owen had not been killed in the war, the kind of poetry developed by Pound and Eliot would have been complemented by an articulate alternative.[1] The point of saying so here is that Pound and Eliot were Americans, and to that extent at a certain distance from English life, while the

[1] John Wain in *The Twentieth-Century Mind* I, 1900–18, ed. Cox and Dyson, p 397.

Georgians were, for better or for worse, English. One critic, for example, has argued that the 'modernist' movement has from the first been mixed up with traits belonging to the specifically American branch of literature in the English language.[2] And in a discussion of some Owen poems in Units 4–5, Arnold Kettle suggests that Owen wrote out of a sense of sharing in common human experiences, as Pound and Eliot tended not to. The issue is complicated, and – to be quite explicit about it – not one to be conducted in chauvinist terms of pro and anti. The simple point is that perhaps the poetic situation in those years was less desperate than Eliot believed.

1.6　And we can add two other reasons for the choice of 1912. The first is that this was the year when Thomas Hardy (1840–1928) began a group of poems which most critics would include in the short list of his greatest lyrics. The date is, as it happens, an accident from the point of view of the literary historian. Hardy was reacting to an event in his private life, not to any general concern for the state of English letters. His poetry, in any case, straddles the 'modernist' revolution, some of it dating from the 1860s, some of it written in the 1920s without any reflection of the new movements. Yet in a general way, Hardy's poetry, a great deal of which *was* written in the period 1900–28, is a major fact in the study of twentieth-century poetry, and that he did write some very impressive poems in 1912 has, from our point of view, a certain symbolic force. One recent critic has gone so far as to suggest that we are wrong to look at the situation solely through the eyes of Pound and Eliot, and that Hardy's poetry, less ambitious in reach, less supported and vindicated by a body of critical thought, has actually been a profounder influence than that of Eliot.[3] It is worth noticing in that connection, that Hardy is not included in John Press's useful anthology, *A Map of Modern English Verse*. There will be some discussion of Hardy's relation to 'modernist' poetry in Units 2–3.

1.7　The second reason concerns the other great poet of the century, W. B. Yeats (1865–1939). Here the story is more complicated. Yeats had been writing since the 1880s, and in 1908 he published an eight-volume *Collected Works* – prose, poetry and plays. To the young Eliot, Yeats belonged to the Victorian past, and as such, was part of a worn out tradition. But Yeats had become discontented with his work. Since about 1903, he had been making radical changes, and he met the young, energetic, immensely self-confident Pound at a moment when his new intentions chimed closely with Pound's ideas. In 1912, Yeats asked Pound to go through his earlier poetry pointing out where it could be improved on the lines of the 'new poetry'. In the same year, he wrote a number of poems which appeared in a volume called *Responsibilities* (1914), where most critics would agree that the new note is unambiguously sounded. We needn't, of course, put too much weight on the actual year. Yeat's poetry developed over several years, and as much by its own internal logic, as by the impact of new trends, but these revisions of Pound's demonstrate that, in his own way, Yeats was struggling with the issues more explicitly illustrated in Pound's and Eliot's work. This point will be looked at more fully in Units 14–15.

1.8　If you have not read much poetry before taking this course, and maybe even if you have, this sketchy touching on large general issues may not make a great deal of sense. Indeed, there is always a strong argument that 'Introductions' to courses properly belong at the end, because only then are they intelligible. Yet I think it may be useful from the start to have a rough idea about why the course begins where it does, and about some connections between the major poets you'll be reading. In the rest of this unit, we are going to look at the kind of poetry that did exist when Eliot and Pound began to write, to provide some kind of framework for understanding later changes. Mainly, that means a discussion of Georgian poetry. But first, I want to look briefly at some examples of the 'new poetry'. You can think of this, perhaps, as a sampling operation to give you some sense of the very varied poetry written in or about 1912.

[2] A. Alvarez *The Shaping Spirit*, p 12.
[3] Donald Davie *Thomas Hardy and British Poetry*, pp 3–12.

2 SOME 'TWENTIETH-CENTURY' POEMS

2.1   I used the term 'modernist' (paras. 1.5 and 1.6) to describe the radical changes coming about in the poetry of the first twenty years of this century. What does it mean? In Units 4–5 *Modernism and Its Origins*, Nick Furbank suggests that 'modernism' is one of those indispensable but elastic concepts like 'Renaissance' or 'Romantic', whose meaning is variously defined by different scholars, and with chronological limits still being debated. If you are particularly curious now, you could turn to the essay in the Course Reader[4], ' "Modern" and "Modernist" ', where the authors argue that 'modernism' describes a deep and general change affecting not only literature, music, painting and sculpture, but philosophy and science as well. Here I offer only the briefest of comments. Critics still use 'modern' and 'modernist' interchangeably (for example, John Press, pp 1–3), but it's surely now more sensible to distinguish them. Over fifty years separates us from the actual events. To identify 'modernist' with 'modern' prevents us asking whether what happened then still exerts essential authority over what is happening today. Perhaps it does. The authors of ' "Modern" and "Modernist" ' argue on those lines. But the question is too important to be obscured by the very terms of the discussion. By and large, then, it seems best to use 'modernism' in a fairly restricted sense to mean the changes affecting poetry (and other arts) in the years 1900–20. What sort of changes were they? I want only to touch on three points. First, an interest in formal experiment, the throwing-off of received patterns and practices, and the beginning again, not from scratch, which is never possible, but by searching for different models, by the conscious adoption of what I called 'new fathers' (1.2). Second, the 'high strenuousness' of much 'modernist' writing, the deep and passionate commitment to the value and importance of literature, and a correspondingly high expectation from readers, to whom 'modernist' poetry makes minimal concessions – one reason why it often seems difficult or obscure. Third, a conscious interest in language, in its nature, in its variousness, in its creative potential. Poets have usually been interested in language, and 'revolutions' in poetry are often associated with new ideas about 'poetic diction' but 'modernist' writing is more sophisticated and more radical in this respect. Here, then, is a group of poems chosen with these three points in mind. They will give the flavour, the accent, of the 'modernist' movement in poetry. Like any short list, it's arbitrary, and I hope you won't use it as an adequate basis for generalizations about 'twentieth-century poetry'. I hope also that you will like these poems. My liking for them has a lot to do with their appearance here. I have added a few questions after each poem, but don't worry about these if you would prefer to read the poems alone, and don't feel you need to read all the poems at a stretch. My own brief comments on the questions come at the end of the whole group (para. 2.15).

2.2   ■ Here is a poem T. S. Eliot wrote in 1911.

> *La Figlia Che Piange*
> O quam te memorem virgo . . .
>
> Stand on the highest pavement of the stair –
> Lean on a garden urn –
> Weave, weave the sunlight in your hair –
> Clasp your flowers to you with a pained surprise –
> Fling them to the ground and turn
> With a fugitive resentment in your eyes:
> But weave, weave the sunlight in your hair.

[4] Graham Martin and P. N. Furbank (eds.) (1975) *Twentieth-Century Poetry: Critical Essays and Documents*, The Open University Press.

9

CHRIST'S COLLEGE
LIBRARY

So I would have had him leave,
So I would have had her stand and grieve,
So he would have left
As the soul leaves the body torn and bruised,
As the mind deserts the body it has used.
I should find
Some way incomparably light and deft,
Some way we both should understand,
Simple and faithless as a smile and shake of the hand.

She turned away, but with the autumn weather
Compelled my imagination many days,
Many days and many hours:
Her hair over her arms and her arms full of flowers.
And I wonder how they should have been together!
I should have lost a gesture and a pose.
Sometimes these cogitations still amaze
The troubled midnight and the noon's repose.

(The title means 'young girl weeping'; the epigraph is part of a sentence from Virgil's *Aeneid* meaning 'Maiden, by what name shall I know you?')

The situation of the first verse might seem traditionally romantic: girl, sun, flowers, garden, and lovers' parting. What is unexpected and unusual about the way the poem develops? When you have thought about that, go on to ask whether the epigraph makes any difference to the poem? Is it merely a display of learning, or does it add interest and meaning? Does the verse form strike you as traditional?

2.3   Eliot also wrote this poem in about 1911.

His soul stretched tight across the skies
That fade behind a city block,
Or trampled by insistent feet
At four and five and six o'clock;
And short square fingers stuffing pipes,
And evening newspapers, and eyes
Assured of certain certainties,
The conscience of a blackened street
Impatient to assume the world.

I am moved by fancies that are curled
Around these images, and cling:
The notion of some infinitely gentle
Infinitely suffering thing.

Wipe your hand across your mouth, and laugh;
The worlds revolve like ancient women
Gathering fuel in vacant lots.

I leave that one to you.

2.4   A poem written by W. B. Yeats in about 1910 is on the next page.

The Cold Heaven

Suddenly I saw the cold and rook-delighting heaven
That seemed as though ice burned and was but the more ice,
And thereupon imagination and heart were driven
So wild that every casual thought of that and this
Vanished, and left but memories, that should be out of season
With the hot blood of youth, of love crossed long ago;
And I took all the blame out of all sense and reason,
Until I cried and trembled and rocked to and fro,
Riddled with light. Ah! when the ghost begins to quicken,
Confusion of the death-bed over, is it sent
Out naked on the roads, as the books say, and stricken
By the injustice of the skies for punishment?

The poet does not go into the particular memories that overwhelm him, but concentrates on what happened when they did. How then does he manage to convey the intensity of his feelings? The end of the poem involves traditional notions about survival after death, but are they *used* traditionally? How would you describe the language of this poem? Ornate, simple, elevated, rich, bare, direct, elaborate . . . ?

2.5   Another poem by Yeats, written in 1913.

The Magi

Now as at all times I can see in the mind's eye,
In their stiff, painted clothes, the pale unsatisfied ones
Appear and disappear in the blue depth of the sky
With all their ancient faces like rain-beaten stones,
And all their helms of silver hovering side by side,
And all their eyes still fixed, hoping to find once more,
Being by Calvary's turbulence unsatisfied,
The uncontrollable mystery on the bestial floor.

Does this poem reflect a traditional view of the Magi?

And how would you describe its language?

2.6   This poem by Yeats was written in 1909.

All Things Can Tempt Me

All things can tempt me from this craft of verse:
One time it was a woman's face, or worse –
The seeming needs of my fool-driven land;
Now nothing but comes readier to the hand
Than this accustomed toil. When I was young,
I had not given a penny for a song
Did not the poet sing it with such airs
That one believed he had a sword upstairs;
Yet would be now, could I but have my wish,
Colder and dumber and deafer than a fish.

Figure 3   W. B. Yeats by I. Opfer, 1935 (National **Portrait** Gallery)

(The third line refers to Yeats' efforts in the cause of Irish nationalism.)

Does this poem indicate that Yeats *has* learnt the 'craft of verse'?

2.7 Ezra Pound published this poem in *Ripostes* (1912).

The Return

See, they return; ah, see the tentative
  Movements, and the slow feet,
    The trouble in the pace and the uncertain
  Wavering!

See, they return, one, and by one,
With fear, as half-awakened;
As if the snow should hesitate
And murmur in the wind,
          and half-turn back;
These were the 'Wing'd-with-Awe',
          Inviolable.

Gods of the wingéd shoe!
With them the silver hounds,
          sniffing the trace of air!

Haie! Haie!
    These were the swift to harry;
These the keen-scented;
These were the souls of blood.

Slow on the leash,
          pallid the leash-men!

Hugh Kenner comments: This verse moves slowly and should be read slowly, with attention to the pointing. It should not be searched for allusions. There is no *external* answer to the man-with-a-notebook's question, 'Who are "They"?' (*The Poetry of Ezra Pound*, p 123). How do the irregular line length and spacing help the verse movement?

2.8 Another Pound poem, also from *Ripostes*.

The Plunge

I would bathe myself in strangeness:
These comforts heaped upon me, smother me!
I burn, I scald so for the new,
New friends, new faces,
Places!
Oh to be out of this,
This that is all I wanted
          – save the new.

And you,
Love, you the much, the more desired!
Do I not loathe all walls, streets, stones,
All mire, mist, all fog,
All ways of traffic?
You, I would have flow over me like water,
Oh, but far out of this!
Grass, and low fields, and hills,
And sun,
Oh, sun enough!
Out, and alone, among some
Alien people!

The rhythms of colloquial speech are sometimes said to be a central feature of the 'new poetry'. Is this true here? Is it altogether true? You could ask the same questions of Eliot's poem in 2.3, and Yeats' in 2.4.

2.9   This poem by Pound was published in *Lustra* (1915).

> *The Coming of War: Actaeon*
>
> An image of Lethe,
>   and the fields
> Full of faint light
>   but golden,
> Gray cliffs,
>   and beneath them
> A sea
> Harsher than granite,
>   unstill, never ceasing;
> High forms
>   with the movement of gods,
> Perilous aspect;
>   And one said:
> 'This is Actaeon.'
>   Actaeon of golden greaves!
> Over fair meadows,
> Over the cool face of that field,
> Unstill, ever moving
> Hosts of an ancient people,
> The silent cortège.

greaves = leg armour

If you don't know about Actaeon or Lethe, don't worry about it. Make what you can of the poem, before turning to my comment. Do you think that Kenner's comment on 'The Return' (2.7) applies here?

2.10   James Joyce (1882–1941) wrote only a few poems, and although we are not going to study him in this course, here are two examples, the first written in 1904, the second in 1906.

> *Tilly*
>
> He travels after a winter sun,
> Urging the cattle along a cold red road,
>
> Calling to them, a voice they know,
> He drives his beasts above Cabra.
>
> The voice tells them home is warm.
> They moo and make brute music with their hoofs.
> He drives them with a flowering branch before him,
> Smoke pluming their foreheads.
>
> Boor, bond of the herd,
> Tonight, stretch full by the fire!
> I bleed by the black stream
> For my torn bough!

I Hear an Army

I hear an army charging upon the land,
And the thunder of horses plunging; foam about their knees.
Arrogant, in black armour, behind them stand,
Disdaining the reins, with fluttering whips, the charioteers.

They cry into the night their battle name:
I moan in sleep when I hear afar their whirling laughter.
They cleave the gloom of dreams, a blinding flame,
Clanging, clanging upon the heart as upon an anvil.

They come shaking in triumph their long green hair:
They come out of the sea and run shouting by the shore.
My heart, have you no wisdom thus to despair?
My love, my love, my love, why have you left me alone?

Only with the last line do you find what the second poem is about. Is it more or less effective for the delay? As with the Yeats poem in 2.4 how does the poet convey the *strength* of his feelings?

2.11   Here is a poem written by Thomas Hardy (1840–1928), probably in about 1910–11, published in *Satires of Circumstance* (1914).

'*Ah, are you digging on my grave?*'

'Ah, are you digging on my grave,
　My loved one? – planting rue?'
– 'No: yesterday he went to wed
One of the brightest wealth has bred.
"It cannot hurt her now," he said,
　"That I should not be true." '

'Then who is digging on my grave?
　My nearest, dearest kin?'
– 'Ah, no: they sit and think, "What use!
What good will planting flowers produce?
No tendance of her mound can loose
　Her spirit from Death's gin." '

'But some one digs upon my grave?
　My enemy? – prodding sly?'
– 'Nay: when she heard you had passed the Gate
That shuts on all flesh soon or late,
She thought you no more worth her hate,
　And cares not where you lie.'

'Then, who is digging on my grave?
　Say – since I have not guessed!'
– 'O it is I, my mistress dear,
Your little dog, who still lives near,
And much I hope my movements here
　Have not disturbed your rest?'

'Ah, yes! *You* dig upon my grave . . .
　Why flashed it not on me
That one true heart was left behind!
What feeling do we ever find
To equal among human kind
　A dog's fidelity.'

14

'Mistress, I dug upon your grave
    To bury a bone, in case
I should be hungry near this spot
When passing on my daily trot.
I am sorry, but I quite forgot
    It was your resting-place.'

What point(s) would you raise about this poem if you were recommending it (or otherwise) to one of next year's students?

2.12 Two more Hardy poems, the first from the winter of 1912–13 just after the death of his first wife, the second in 1884.

The Walk

    You did not walk with me
    Of late to the hill-top tree
        By the gated ways,
        As in earlier days;
        You were weak and lame,
        So you never came,
    And I went alone, and I did not mind,
    Not thinking of you as left behind.

    I walked up there to-day
    Just in the former way;
        Surveyed around
        The familiar ground
        By myself again:
        What difference, then?
    Only that underlying sense
    Of the look of a room on returning thence.

A Countenance

Her laugh was not in the middle of her face quite,
    As a gay laugh springs,
It was plain she was anxious about some things
    I could not trace quite.
Her curls were like fir-cones – piled up, brown –
    Or rather like tight-tied sheaves:
It seemed they could never be taken down . . .

And her lips were too full, some might say:
I did not think so. Anyway,
The shadow her lower one would cast
Was green in hue whenever she passed
    Bright sun on midsummer leaves.
Alas, I knew not much of her,
And lost all sight and touch of her!

If otherwise, should I have minded
The shy laugh not in the middle of her face quite,
And would my kisses have died of drouth quite
    As love became unblinded?

What is your impression of the language of these poems?

2.13   D. H. Lawrence (1885–1931), like Joyce better known as a novelist than a poet, nevertheless wrote a great deal of poetry. He published 'All Souls' in *Look We Have Come Through* (1913) and I have included it here, although Lawrence's poetry is not discussed in depth in the course. The poem refers to his mother who died in 1911.

All Souls

They are chanting now the service of All the Dead
And the village folk outside in the burying-ground
Listen – except those who strive with their dead,
Reaching out in anguish, yet unable quite to touch them:
Those villagers isolated at the grave
Where the candles burn in the daylight, and the painted wreaths
Are propped on end, there, where the mystery starts.

The naked candles burn on every grave.
On your grave, in England, the weeds grow.

But I am your naked candle burning,
And that is not your grave, in England,
The world is your grave.
And my naked body standing on your grave
Upright towards heaven is burning off to you
Its flame of life, now and always, till the end.

It is my offering to you: every day is All Soul's Day.

I forget you, have forgotten you.
I am busy only at my burning,
I am busy only at my life.
But my feet are on your grave, planted.
And when I lift my face, it is a flame that goes up
To the other world, where you are now.
But I am not concerned with you.
    I have forgotten you.

I am a naked candle burning on your grave.

How would you describe the language of this poem? Do you see a resemblance between its rhythm and that of Pound's in 2.7?

2.14   Finally, an early poem by Eliot, from about 1911, but not published till 1967 in *Poems Written in Early Youth*.

The Death of Saint Narcissus

    Come under the shadow of this gray rock –
Come in under the shadow of this gray rock,
And I will show you something different from either
Your shadow sprawling over the sand at daybreak, or
Your shadow leaping behind the fire against the red rock:
I will show you his bloody cloth and limbs
And the gray shadow on his lips.

    He walked once between the sea and the high cliffs
When the wind made him aware of his limbs smoothly passing each other
And of his arms crossed over his breast.
When he walked over the meadows
He was stifled and soothed by his own rhythm.

By the river
His eyes were aware of the pointed corners of his eyes
And his hands aware of the pointed tips of his fingers.

Struck down by such knowledge
He could not live men's ways, but became a dancer before God
If he walked in city streets
He seemed to tread on faces, convulsive thighs and knees.
So he came out under the rock.

    First he was sure that he had been a tree,
Twisting its branches among each other
And tangling its roots among each other.

    Then he knew that he had been a fish
With slippery white belly held tight in his own fingers,
Writhing in his own clutch, his ancient beauty
Caught fast in the pink tips of his new beauty.

    Then he had been a young girl
Caught in the woods by a drunken old man
Knowing at the end the taste of his own whiteness
The horror of his own smoothness,
And he felt drunken and old.

    So he became a dancer to God.
Because his flesh was in love with the burning arrows
He danced on the hot sand
Until the arrows came.
As he embraced them his white skin surrendered itself to the redness of
    blood, and satisfied him.
Now he is green, dry and stained
With the shadow in his mouth.

Discussion

2.15 Some brief comments to test your own against.

2.2 The poem develops unexpectedly because it is not clear whether the situation in the first verse actually happened; the second verse suggests that it might have, but didn't ('so I *would have* had him leave'). Real and imagined events are interfused. The epigraph doesn't matter a great deal, but pinpoints the poem's main area of uncertainty. The irregular line lengths, the lack of pattern in the verses, and in the rhymes, is 'modernist'. (See Units 4–5, Section 6.)

2.4 Light imagery conveys the intense pain of the memory, as does the notion of excruciatingly cold ice. The idea of the 'ghost', or spirit, wandering the roads, punished by its nakedness to the heavens, like a beggar, seems to me a brilliantly original adaptation of conventional ideas about the afterlife. The words are plain and straightforward, but the syntax, the sentence structure, is elaborate.

2.5 The language is more magnificent, the tone elevated, mysterious. Notice that the poem is one long sentence ('I can see . . . the pale unsatisfied ones . . .' etc.). Again, Yeats takes over a traditional notion from several famous Renaissance paintings (we have all seen them in Christmas card form at least) of the Adoration of the Magi, and gives it an astonishing application. These Magi have observed not Christ's birth but his crucifixion, and they long for something else. What? The poem leaves you with that sinister enigma.

2.6   It seems to me a highly accomplished little poem: both patterned and easy in manner. Read it out loud if you are not sure about this.

2.7   The spacing and line lengths slow you down as you read; it's natural to pause in between line breaks; also the eye needs a moment to take in the differently placed half-lines.

2.8   It combines the movement of natural speech, with subtle interruptions and emphases, and occasional lines of heightened rhythm. For example, 'You, I would have flow over me like water' followed by the more colloquial 'Oh, but far out of this'. Eliot's and Yeats's poems show the same kind of thing, more emphatically. So does Lawrence's.

2.9   Lethe is the name of a river in Hades, and therefore associated with death. Actaeon was a Greek warrior. A myth relates that he spied on Diana, the goddess of hunting, while she was bathing, and she revenged herself by setting her fierce hunting dogs on him, tearing him to pieces. I think all you need to know for this poem is that he was a Greek warrior who died. Kenner's comment on 'The Return' also applies here.

2.10   The last line of Joyce's 'I Hear an Army' is effective where it is, because the preceding images convey the actual quality and depth of feeling that the question ('why have you left me alone?') cannot do. The method resembles Yeats's in 'The Cold Heaven'.

2.11   I would make two points: the sardonic humour (the poem relates a conversation between a dead person and a dog); and the clever use of the verse form which advances the story, and leads neatly to the final revelation.

2.12   The language is, on the whole, simple, direct, unadorned, yet eloquent and moving. The second poem uses the kind of real speech in its first line that you might think hopelessly awkward, yet here it becomes expressive and subtle, and combines well with the richer language of the second verse (look at the first three lines), and of the last. I include it partly for its date, 1884, though Hardy did not publish it till 1928. It suggests how individual Hardy's writing was, and how he anticipated one aspect of the 'new poetry'.

2.13   The tone of Lawrence's language is remarkably direct and straightforward, yet it moves towards heightened poetic effects. He develops the candle/grave motif from a description in the first verse into a brilliant metaphor for the relation between the living and the dead in the last line. The connection with Pound's poem is that both use unrhymed verse, building a rhythmical shape out of single lines (Lawrence doesn't use half-lines) of different lengths. ■

2.16   You may find it useful to look at these poems again after reading Units 4–5. Here are the references.

Eliot *Collected Poems 1909–1962*, pp 36, 24–5.
Eliot *Poems Written in Early Youth*, pp 34–5.
Yeats *Collected Poems*, pp 140, 141, 109.
Pound *Collected Shorter Poems*, pp 85, 82, 117.
The Essential James Joyce (ed. H. Levin), p 341.
The Complete Poems of D. H. Lawrence (ed. V. de Sola Pinto and F. W. Roberts), p 233.
Hardy *Collected Poems*, pp 310–11.
Poems of Thomas Hardy: A New Selection (ed. Creighton), pp 51, 114.

3 POETIC DICTION: 'VICTORIAN' AND 'TWENTIETH-CENTURY'

THE REACTION AGAINST VICTORIAN POETRY

3.1 The 'modernist' poets explicitly broke with the main poetic influences flowing from the Victorian period. Eliot turned to the *symboliste* writing of the French poet Jules Laforgue (1860–87), and to earlier English poetry, Jacobean dramatic verse and the metaphysical poems of John Donne (1572–1631) and his seventeenth-century followers. Pound looked for even earlier models in thirteenth-century Provençal lyrics and in the Italian Guido Calvacanti (1259–1300). But their dissatisfaction with recent English poetry was not in itself new. Since the 1890s, and with gathering intensity, a reaction had built up against certain 'Victorian' notions about the language and subject matter of poetry. Yeats, for example, had objected to the explicit moralizing, lazy poeticisms, and rhetorical uplift of much Victorian writing. Early in this century he began to practise a more colloquial idiom, and a less 'poetic' voice. Here is a poem he published in 1905.

Never Give All The Heart

Never give all the heart, for love
Will hardly seem worth thinking of
To passionate women if it seem
Certain, and they never dream
That it fades out from kiss to kiss;
For everything that's lovely is
A brief, dreamy, kind delight.
O never give the heart outright,
For they, for all smooth lips can say,
Have given their hearts up to the play.
And who could play it well enough
If deaf and dumb and blind with love?
He that made this knows all the cost,
For he gave all his heart and lost.

Notice how direct the opening tone of voice is, how simple the language, close to ordinary speech, and how the sense flows over the line-endings, so that while we register the fact of the rhymes (love/of, seem/dream, kiss/is, etc.) they do not cut the sentences up into obviously rhymed couplets. And the lover conveys his feeling of utter loss, not through direct emotional claims, but by a combination of argument ('passionate women' think of love as a game that necessarily ends; the wholly-committed lover is bound to play such a game badly) and reserved understatement (the impersonality of 'He that made this . . .', i.e. the writer of the poem).

3.2 ■ I want now to look in greater detail at these points about poetic language. Here are two poems about winter. Read them carefully, say how you think they differ, what impression each poet was after, and how each uses language to convey it. Which poem do you prefer?

Winter: East Anglia

In a frosty sunset
    So fiery red with cold
The footballer's onset
    Rings out glad and bold;

19

Then boys from daily tether
  With famous dogs at heel
In starlight meet together
  And to farther hedges steal;
Where the rats are pattering
  In and out the stacks,
Owls with hatred chattering
  Swoop at the terriers' backs.
And, frost forgot, the chase grows hot
  Till a rat's a foolish prize,
But the cornered weasel stands his ground,
Shrieks at the dogs and boys set round,
Shrieks as he knows they stand all round,
  And hard as winter dies.

A Wintry Picture

Now where the bare sky spans the landscape bare,
Up long brown fallows creeps the slow brown team,
Scattering the seed-corn that must sleep and dream,
Till by Spring's carillon awakened there.
Ruffling the tangles of his thicket hair,
The stripling yokel steadies now the beam,
Now strides erect with cheeks that glow and gleam,
And whistles shrewdly to the spacious air.
Lured onward to the distance dim and blear,
The road crawls weary of the travelled miles:
The kine stand cowering in unmoving files;
The shrewmouse rustles through the bracken sere;
And, in the sculptured woodland's leafless aisles,
The robin chants the vespers of the year.

kine = cattle
files = rows
sere = withered

Discussion

3.3 The first poem mainly describes a human activity, and the second concentrates on scenery, but I think we can usefully contrast them as attempts to say something about winter. The point of the first poem lies, wouldn't you say, in the last line. Winter is 'hard', and by that the poet means savage and cruel. The hunting of the rats and weasels represents the real meaning of winter. The observed scene is not 'scenery', not a seasonal aspect of nature, which men can observe, and then withdraw from into their human world, but a recurring expression of what, together, man and nature are: destructive. The language is economical and straightforward, and the form of the poem, with its short abrupt lines and simple rhyming scheme, is unremarkable until the last four lines, where the longer lines and repeated rhyme word (ground/round/round) reflect the mounting excitement of the successful hunt. The poet does not tell us what he feels or thinks about the situation, but concentrates on presenting it in such a way as to imply his feeling.

The point of the second poem is, I feel, to convey a literary man's impression of winter. It conjures an atmosphere, rather than presents a memorable scene. Or perhaps one should say that it evokes feelings that derive more from other poems, or from language we respond to as 'poetic', rather than from immediate observation. Look at the last two lines. 'Sculptured' is really a very strange way to *describe* leafless trees. It seems to have been indirectly suggested by the familiar notion that a wood is like a Gothic church. In the same way, the robin's song has been turned into 'vespers', formal religious singing. Think about that for a moment. Earlier, there is the phrase 'Spring's carillon' (a carillon is a melody played on bells) and the seeds are said to be 'dreaming'. Actual spring, the actual germination of seeds, are removed to a considerable distance by language like this. Some of the detail, certainly, is different: the first two lines, perhaps, or the one about the shrewmouse. But the ploughman remains a vague impression to me, a literary convention only. Even the vivid detail we are given like 'whistles shrewdly to the spacious air', is puzzling rather than anything else. What does it mean to whistle 'shrewdly'? Formally, the second poem is a sonnet. Something I like about the poem is the rhythm which is smooth and pleasing, giving a not unsuccessful mood of calm and quiet. The writing has an air of assurance that perhaps belongs to the successful managing of a traditional form like the sonnet.■

I don't know which poem you preferred. The question in any case brings up the difficult business of 'value judgements'. Are these merely expressions of personal caprice? Can they be discussed? Is there any point in elaborating the reasons for liking one poem rather than another? Here, I'd make two comments. First, poems (just as much as novels and plays) invite you to make value judgements about human experience. Full response to them means, in some way, assenting to, or dissenting from, the 'value' they offer. Poems implicitly say, 'Isn't this interesting, important, valuable, etc.?' A full reading means deciding whether or not you agree, and that brings into play *your* conception of what is or is not valuable. Second, working out your reasons for liking or disliking poems both helps you to clarify to yourself how you are making your judgements, and directly assists the process of interaction between yourself and the poem that can *change* your sense of the valuable. 'Judging poems' is not altogether the judicial process it sounds like, a testing of poems against a set of abstract standards, but more a creative exploration of your and the poem's notions of what is valuable. Poems 'judge' readers quite as much as the other way round.

To go back to these two poems about winter. I like them both in different ways, but I prefer the first. It says something about human experience that I find interesting, and the poet uses the various tricks of poetic language (rhythm, rhyme, and so forth) to convey that insight, not to impress me with his professional skill as a writer. The second lacks that kind of meaning. More in the nature of a performance, it invites attention to itself as a skilful manipulation of 'poetic' effects. Skilful performance, a feature of all art, is certainly admirable in itself. But the same could be said about juggling, where the only thing you *can* admire is the performer's skill. Now there *are* poems that ask only that you should enjoy their verbal dexterity. But the second poem is, I think, pretending that its 'technical' skill adds up to something more, rather as if a juggler were to insist that his agility conveyed some sensitive comment on human life. My reason for feeling this lies in the failure of the poem's language to convey a direct experience of its subject. Something in its style *pretends* to meanings that it does not deliver. Perhaps the poet had less to say than he supposed. Perhaps he accommodated what he wanted to say to a received 'literary' way of saying it. Perhaps he used this slightly inflated language to make his own experience sound more interesting than it was (a temptation, incidentally, very easy to give way to). But for whatever reason, I can only like the second poem as a capable exercise in a conventional manner, whereas the first poem communicates something new; or at least something not unfamiliar, but in a way that makes me think freshly about its importance.

3.4 ■ Compare these two poems in the same way.

The Kingfisher

It was the Rainbow gave thee birth,
   And left thee all her lovely hues;
And, as her mother's name was Tears,
   So runs it in thy blood to choose
For haunts the lonely pools, and keep
In company with trees that weep.

Go you and, with such glorious hues,
   Live with proud Peacocks in green parks;
On lawns as smooth as shining glass,
   Let every feather show its marks;
Get thee on boughs and clap thy wings
   Before the windows of proud kings.

Nay, lovely Bird, thou art not vain;
   Thou hast no proud, ambitious mind;
I also love a quiet place
   That's green, away from all mankind;
A lonely pool, and let a tree
Sigh with her bosom over me.

Humming-bird

I can imagine, in some other world
Primeval-dumb, far back
In that most awful stillness, that only gasped and hummed,
Humming-birds raced down the avenues.

Before anything had a soul,
While life was a heave of Matter, half inanimate,
This little bit chipped off in brilliance
And went whizzing through the slow, vast, succulent stems.

I believe there were no flowers then,
In the world where the humming-bird flashed ahead of creation.
I believe he pierced the slow vegetable veins with his long beak.

Probably he was big
As mosses, and little lizards, they say, were once big.
Probably he was a jabbing, terrifying monster.

We look at him through the wrong end of the long telescope of Time,
Luckily for us.

Discussion

3.5 Both poets write about a bird, but the first is surely much less interested in his ostensible subject than the second. I get only the vaguest impression of what a kingfisher looks like from 'rainbow', or 'lovely hues'. Isn't the first poet's real concern to associate himself with the kingfisher's supposed fondness for lonely places (yet kingfishers mate like other birds), and to make this state of affairs *morally admirable*? The kingfisher is, I feel, a peg on which hangs a little sermon about ambition and modesty, pride and self-abnegation. The tone is strangely oratorical ('go you', 'nay, lovely bird'), and the emotion is conveyed not by presenting us with a situation that evokes a particular range of feelings (as in 'Winter: East Anglia'), but through emotionally-loaded words ('glorious', 'lovely', 'proud', 'lonely'). It is also a 'literary' poem in the sense that it relies on a tradition established mainly by Wordsworth, to the effect that solitary communings with nature are moving and admirable. Perhaps they are. But this poet hardly earns the right to call on that tradition. His own sense of an actual scene is too weak. Look at the second verse. How could a small bird 'clap' its wings? Or again, in the third verse, the bosomed sighing tree. Such language does not suggest that the poet has some particular experience of his own to convey. The poem communicates a feeling, certainly, but it seems to me vague, generalized, secondhand.

The second poet is ostensibly concerned to 'imagine' what a humming-bird might have been like at an early stage of its evolution. Its speed, how it ate, its long sharp beak, and its original size all suggest how terrifyingly different things may have been. The tone combines a sense of wonder, with a deliberate undercutting of possible solemnity. Thus, the first verse conveys awe, even fear, while words like 'raced', 'whizzed', 'jabbing' contribute a more down-to-earth note, and the last two lines are colloquial ('Luckily for us'), with half-humorous effect. But as a whole it communicates perhaps something more general than an imaginary version of primeval humming-birds, and that is an evocation of nature's distinctly non-human order. The poet may seem to distance us from this idea by setting the scene in primeval times, but he 'imagines' it so powerfully that surely it challenges us to think again about our own relation with nature, how human concepts like 'soul' or 'mind' are related to the living energies that account for evolution.

What did you think of each poem? You will have sensed, I dare say, that I prefer the second, and rather more emphatically than in the previous comparison, though for similar reasons. Another way of stating my preference would be to contrast the form of each poem. The first uses a pattern of rhymes and stanzas that are, in themselves, shaped and regular, and the tone tries to be elevated and high-sounding, but there is almost nothing *in* the poem to justify this. The poet uses the 'form' to eke out the slenderness of his 'meaning'. He provides an elaborate formal dress for an idea and a feeling that are in themselves commonplace, secondhand. But the second poet has found a form that reflects the complex of feelings he wants to convey about the primeval world. Abandoning rhyme and set stanzas does not mean his poem has no form. On the contrary, it allows him a valuable flexibility, a rhythmic 'shape' more sensitive to the inner meaning. This kind of verse is known as *vers libre* but the use of it here illustrates Eliot's remark 'no verse is *libre* for the man who wants to do a good job'. The 'freedom' this poet enjoys is a discipline of its own.■

3.6 ■ Now compare these two poems in the same way.

A Passer-By

Whither, O splendid ship, thy white sails crowding,
  Leaning across the bosom of the urgent West,
That fearest nor sea rising, nor sky clouding,
  Whither away, fair rover, and what thy quest?
  Ah! soon, when Winter has all our vales opprest,
When skies are cold and misty, and hail is hurling,
  Wilt thou glide on the blue Pacific, or rest
In a summer haven asleep, thy white sails furling.

23

I there before thee, in the country that thou well knowest,
   Already arrived am inhaling thy odorous air:
I watch thee unerringly where thou goest,
   And anchor queen of the strange shipping there,
   Thy sails for awnings spread, thy masts bare;
Nor is aught from the foaming reef to the snow-capp'd, grandest
   Peak, that is over the feathery plains, more fair
Than thou, so upright, so stately, and still thou standest.

And yet, O splendid ship, unhail'd and nameless,
   I know not, if, aiming a fancy, I rightly divine
That thou hast a purpose joyful, a courage blameless,
   Thy port assured in a happier land than mine.
   But for all I have given thee, beauty enough is thine,
As thou, aslant with trim tackle and shrouding,
   From the proud nostril curve of a prow's line
In the offing scatterest foam, thy white sails crowding.

In Harbour

Surely there, among the great docks, is peace,
   my mind;
there with the ships moored in the river.
Go out, timid child,
and snuggle in among the great ships talking so
   quietly.
Maybe you will even fall asleep near them and be
lifted into one of their laps, and in the morning –
There is always the morning in which to remember
   it all!
Of what are they gossiping? God knows.
And God knows it matters little for we cannot
   understand them.
Yet it is certainly of the sea, of that there can be
   no question.
It is a quiet sound. Rest! That's all I care for now
The smell of them will put us to sleep presently.
Smell! It is the sea water mingling here into the
   river –
at least so it seems – perhaps it is something else –
   but what matter?
The sea water! It is quiet and smooth here!
How slowly they move, little by little trying
the hawsers that drop and groan with their agony.
Yes, it is certainly of the high sea they are talking.

What these poems are about is less immediately clear than in the previous cases. When you have read them once, or perhaps twice, try to pin this down in a couple of sentences. In the second poem, 'timid child' (line 3) refers to the poet's own mind.

Discussion

3.7 I have a mixed reaction to both poems, and find it hard to choose between them. 'A Passer-By' is written in the style that I have called 'literary' (3.3). It is full of words not used in normal speech ('whither', 'thy', 'aught', 'rightly divine'), old-fashioned verbal forms ('fearest', 'knowest'), and its rhymed and formal stanzas, its rhetorical questions and evocations ('O splendid ship') aim at a lofty 'poetic' tone. Certainly it sustains the manner more successfully than 'The Kingfisher'. The questions the poet asks are, on the whole, right for this tone of address. I do not feel any ludicrous disparity between 'form' and 'meaning' in that respect. Yet it is often remarkably vague. In the second verse, doesn't one want to know why this ship is 'queen' over the others? And why are the other ships in the foreign port any more 'strange' than this one? Is there a hidden assumption that it is English and therefore rules the ocean? And the geography of the last three lines of this verse is very mysterious. . . . Or in the third verse, it is suggested that the ship stands for a quality of life the poet can only imagine: beauty, courage, purpose and joy. Yet does his account of the ship communicate these qualities with any force or particularity? He seems to me to lean heavily on a 'travel poster' image of a ship in full sail, and the idea that the port it is bound for is 'happier' is a mere assertion. Romantic poetry stands at the back of this poem too, the formal odes of Keats and Shelley, but there is an independent energy and conviction in its rhythms, which I find attractive.

The second poem is strikingly different in language, tone and form. There are no rhymes, or stanza form, and only the rhythmic movement of *vers libre*. The tone is conversational, direct and the situation definite enough: the moored ships, quiet water, sea smell, creaking hawsers. But the meaning is surely rather elusive. Why is the sea attractive? Seemingly because it offers rest and peace, but is the poet saying that his feeling about it is infantile, a psychological regression (the ships are seen as parents), or is it a desirable freedom? Does he present either possibility with interesting vigour? I think this poem 'pretends' to meanings that the poet cannot decide about. The fluid rhythms convey rather well the kind of feeling he has about the sea, but he seems unable to make up his mind what this feeling amounts to. As in 'A Wintry Picture', the 'meaning' has been spread thin. The style allows the poet to sound speculative and mysterious, when in fact he is really indecisive. Or so I feel.■

3.8   Here are the authors and dates of publication of the poems.

3.2   'Winter: East Anglia', Edmund Blunden (b. 1896), 1920.
      'A Wintry Picture', Alfred Austin (1835–1913), 1885.

3.4   'The Kingfisher', W. H. Davies (1871–1940), 1911.
      'Humming-bird', D. H. Lawrence (1885–1931), 1923.

3.6   'A Passer-By', Robert Bridges (1844–1930), 1880.
      'In Harbour', William Carlos Williams (1883–1963), 1930.

3.9   The discussion of these pairs of poems had two purposes. One was to provide an early opportunity to look closely at some poems, and to suggest that though critical judgement is in the end a personal matter, there are ways of discussing one's preferences, and that it is helpful to do so. The study of poetry is first and foremost the study of particular poems, and that should always mean, at some point, trying to decide which poems matter to you. There is no 'right' answer. Nobody's answer can be *proved*. But one way of communicating and exploring critical judgements is to ask what the poet is doing with the words he uses: what effects is he aiming at, what particular experience is he trying to convey, how far has he achieved an adequate language for his perceptions. These are questions to ask of every poem you read.

The second purpose you may have guessed from the dates of publication. I wanted to bring out the kind of objections to Victorian poetry that became widely current in the first decade of this century. 'A Wintry Picture', 'The Kingfisher', 'A Passer-By' illustrate the kind of poetic language 'twentieth-century' poets disliked: a consciously 'literary' diction; a special 'poetic' tone of voice; heavy reliance on second-hand stylistic effects in verse form and verse rhythm, usually at the expense of the declared subject matter; the practice of evoking feeling through emotionally-loaded words rather than through the presentation of particular experiences. 'Winter: East Anglia', 'Humming-bird', and 'In Harbour' show the opposite traits: a good deal of ordinary language, no automatically 'poetic' voice, no mechanical eloquence, the use of colloquial speech rhythms, an evocation of feeling and idea from specific situations; a more flexible and adventurous use of poetic forms and a greater concern to make 'style' (the way something is said) directly reflect 'content' (what is said).

POETIC STYLE

3.10   Generalizations about period 'styles' always need qualification, and these are no exception. First, what the three 'Victorian' poems represent is *not* the poetry of the Victorian period but its weaker side, which lay in its conception of 'the poetic' – of what poetic subjects were, and what poetic language had to be. By the end of the century, this had become an oppressive tradition, though quite why the varied riches of Romantic and Victorian poetry had shrunk to an influence felt to be narrow and stifling is a large and difficult question, which we can hardly go into in this course. But you will find discussions of it in two of the set books, F. R. Leavis, *New Bearings in English Poetry*, pp 7–21, and C. K. Stead, *The New Poetic*, pp 44–66. Second, the fact that the 'twentieth-century' group of poems share a plain low-key conversational manner should not be taken to imply either that this in itself is an unmistakable sign of 'twentieth-century' writing, or that it is an infallible recipe for successful poems. (That is why I included 'In Harbour'.) The point to be clear about is that any period 'style' encourages certain kinds of poem, and discourages others. What is more characteristic of twentieth-century poems is a fondness for combining a plain and heightened language in the same poem. Lawrence's 'Humming-bird' shows something of this, and you'll meet many more examples in Hardy, Yeats, Eliot and Pound. By incorporating a plain style into its conception of 'the poetic', twentieth-century poets added to the kinds of language a poet could use, and so to the kinds of experience he could write about. Third, though there *was* a strong reaction against the 'dream world' tendency and the would-be lofty language of the poems by Austin, Davies and Bridges, that is not because twentieth-century poets lacked imaginative energy or the ability to write with magnificence. Far from it. But they needed first to create new forms for the poetic imagination, and that meant clearing away the older models. You can briefly remind yourself of what that meant in practice by looking again at some of the poems in Section 2 (e.g. Yeats' 'The Magi', Pound's 'The Coming of War: Actaeon', Eliot's 'The Death of Saint Narcissus').

Yeats was not the only poet interested in a barer poetic style. Some of his contemporaries in the 1890s, poets like Ernest Dowson (1867–1900), or John Davidson (1857–1909) whose fine ballad 'Thirty Bob A Week' helped Eliot's search for a language closer to common speech, shared the conviction that the large-gestured 'Victorian' manner had become an impediment. The same seems to have been true of Thomas Hardy whose career can be said to stand as a sardonic admonishment against the literary historian's busy concern with patterns and trends. Hardy only began to publish poetry in 1898. But he had already written a great deal, and if you look again at 'A Countenance' (2.12), written in 1884, you'll see how utterly un-'Victorian' it is. It is as if Hardy had personally invented 'twentieth-century style' and then put it away in his desk drawer till the right time came round. There is the fidelity to a particular experience, the slightness of the remembered incident, the subtly varied use of ordinary speech rhythms, even the playing-off of plain against more heightened styles. Hardy published volumes in 1902 and 1909, so it is not surprising that his influence helped poets of the Georgian movement in their reaction against the past.

A. E. HOUSMAN

3.11 Something should also be said about another poet who cannot be accused of the 'Victorian' style in any obvious way, yet who published his first volume in the Victorian period, *The Shropshire Lad* (1896). A. E. Housman (1859–1936), a brilliant Latin scholar by profession, wrote, mainly under the impetus of a frustrated love for another man, a body of short lyrics highly regarded in the Edwardian period for their spare language, strict regard for verse form – though of a simple kind – and song-like qualities. For example:

> Loveliest of trees, the cherry now
> Is hung with bloom along the bough
> And stands about the woodland ride
> Wearing white for Eastertide.
>
> Now of my threescore years and ten,
> Twenty will not come again,
> And take from seventy springs a score,
> It only leaves me fifty more.
>
> And since to look at things in bloom
> Fifty springs are little room,
> About the woodlands I will go
> To see the cherry hung with snow.

The language is simple – in a sense. No expansive gestures or rhythms, no vaguely emotional words. The poem has a satisfying neatness of form, and a certain charm, with its playful calculation in the second verse, and attractive insistence that fifty years is too short a time to appreciate the cherry blossom. Yet I have a reservation about it, not unlike my reaction to some of the poems we have just been discussing. Think about it yourself. You may not share such feelings, nor do I want to suggest that you ought to. But as an exercise, do you see any resemblance between this poem and an aspect of 'A Wintry Picture', 'The Kingfisher', 'A Passer-By' and 'In Harbour'?

3.12 Here is a more personal poem, resembling Hardy's 'The Walk' (2.12) in speaking directly about an actual incident.

> Because I liked you better
>   Than suits a man to say,
> It irked you, and I promised
>   To throw the thought away.
>
> To put the world between us
>   We parted, stiff and dry;
> 'Goodbye', said you, 'forget me.'
>   'I will, no fear', said I.
>
> If here, where clover whitens
>   The dead man's knoll, you pass,
> And no tall flower to meet you
>   Starts in the trefoiled grass,
>
> Halt by the headstone naming
>   The heart no longer stirred,
> And say the lad that loved you
>   Was one that kept his word.

trefoil = clover

Figure 4   A. E. Housman by W. Rothenstein, 1906 (National Portrait Gallery)

CHRIST'S COLLEGE LIBRARY

And a third Housman poem:

> Others, I am not the first,
> Have willed more mischief than they durst:
> If in the breathless night I too
> Shiver now, 'tis nothing new.
>
> More than I, if truth were told,
> Have stood and sweated hot and cold,
> And through their reins in ice and fire
> Fear contended with desire.
>
> Agued once like me were they,
> But I like them shall win my way
> Lastly to the bed of mould
> Where there's neither heat nor cold.
>
> But from my grave across my brow
> Plays no wind of healing now,
> And fire and ice within me fight
> Beneath the suffocating night.

reins = loins

■ Compare this with the previous poem as two attempts to express painful feeling. Which do you prefer, and why? Remember again there's no 'right' answer, but explaining your preference helps to deepen your own response, whatever it happens to be.

Discussion

3.13 My reservation about the first poem is that the charm is a little selfconscious, the simplicity a little too carefully cultivated. As a decorative remark about cherry blossoms, I wonder if 'Wearing white for Eastertide' really helps the poet with his main idea. Do associations with the Christian festival, or with Easter brides, sharpen one's impression of the blossom? 'Cherry hung with snow' seems equally off-beam. Snow can hardly be said to 'hang' from the boughs it lies on? The poet is using only part of the word's meaning, and the obvious part, its colour. Such language seems to me to lack the pressure of an individual experience, and in this poem that surely should mean conveying not just the whiteness, but the freshness, the lightness, the movement, of the flowers. (Poems, successful in this respect, that you might like to compare with Housman's, are Pound's 'In a Station of the Metro' (1.3), and Hardy's 'Snow in the Suburbs' (*Poems of Thomas Hardy, A New Selection*, ed. Creighton, p 11).) The way the poet describes the cherry blossoms does not sufficiently 'carry' the value he claims to put on seeing it. So his argument about it seems, in the end, overdone.. This is the point of contact with earlier poems we have discussed. The poem 'pretends' to a meaning it does not convey. I'm conscious, nevertheless, that I may be making too much of this. A colleague in the course team remarked: 'I think you're rather unfair here: you assume that Housman's interest is in "conveying an experience", whereas I see the poem more as a brief meditation on time. Also, "Wearing white for Eastertide" seems a reasonable line to me because of the association of Easter with regeneration, which relates to the passage of time and growing older.' How did you feel yourself?

I think the second poem begins well. The stiff-upper-lip note of the first two verses seems exactly right for the stoic suppression of the feelings that had to be suppressed by their very nature. (Oscar Wilde, remember, was tried and convicted in 1895 on account of the 'love that dare not speak its name'.) The second half is certainly moving, but I find myself pausing over the word 'lad'. Housman was fond of using it, and when he writes about fictional young men from Shropshire who fall foul of the law or are jilted by their girls, it works well enough. But here, in a more personal poem, it strikes a wrong note. 'Housman', I find myself saying, 'isn't a "lad", he's an adult, a scholar and writer in late-nineteenth-century English society.' Is it a covert way of referring to a homosexual love? Perhaps. Yet there seems also an element of poetic attitudinizing. Suppose one substitutes 'chap' for 'lad'. Doesn't that highlight a certain artificiality in the poem's feeling? Or again, substitute 'man'. Also, that shift from the abrupt parting of the friends to the imagined scene of the speaker's grave trembles on the verge of the theatrical. Instead of the living pain, we are given the fiction of a nobly-faithful death intended to impress the lost lover – and the reader – with the cost of keeping the promise.

That's where I prefer the third poem. Notice how the poet's feelings are introduced in the context of a general human experience, so that we move towards the final verse without any suggestion of self-advertising, of the poet making public virtue out of his private pain. Anybody might feel like me, he says, and many have. In the second poem, perhaps because, homosexuality being a taboo subject, the feelings cannot be fully explored, there is a sense of evasion. But the third finds words and images ('fire and ice') which speak directly enough, yet also generally about a conflict of feelings that has to be suffered because it cannot be resolved. One believes in that 'suffocating night', both as actual scene and as a revealing metaphor. I would sum up my preference for the third poem by saying that it is more honest than the second, more concerned to say completely what the experience is and less caught up in moral self-dramatization. ∎

3.14 These poems by Housman, then, should remind us that a relatively unadorned language and relatively straightforward poetic form (compared with, say, the poem by Bridges 'A Passer-By', 3.6) aren't necessarily free from the impulse to decorate experiences in an acceptably 'literary' way. Hardy's directness is an achievement Housman cannot match, perhaps because of personal factors, but also because, one is inclined to think, of the powerful influence of the idea that poems ought to be 'poetic' (as in 'Loveliest of trees'), ought in some way to furbish ordinary experience, and make it look more impressive. Doubtless this tendency is always at work, and I do not want to suggest that you couldn't find many poems in our century in which a later 'style' is used to dress up, or in some other way disguise, the poet's experience. Indeed, as I have already suggested, 'In Harbour' (3.6) may be such a poem. Hardy and Housman were important to the Georgian poets partly because they cultivated a simpler, directer poetic diction, partly because they were more 'realistic' in their subject matter. But there's more than one kind of 'simplicity', and of 'realism', and in looking at influences, we need to keep this in mind.

4.1   As we have seen, Georgian poetry took its name from George V's accession to the throne in 1910. Today, we distinguish the Edwardian from the Victorian periods, but during the opening years of this century 'Victorianism' must have seemed very much alive. Victoria herself died in 1901, and Edward VII, the new king, had long been a familiar figure. A more significant break with the previous century came in 1906 when the first Liberal Government for many years made inroads into the political dominance of the Conservative party and the landed aristocracy, reflected in the Lloyd George 'People's' Budget of 1909, which first introduced welfare measures like a national insurance scheme, and first taxed inherited wealth with an estate duty. The election of a second Liberal Government in 1910 led to a confrontation with the House of Lords whose legislative powers were drastically curtailed in the Parliament Bill of 1911. So the term 'Georgian' associated the new poetry with the future, as against the past, with a general current of reform. For some years too, there had been a vigorous anti-Victorian movement in other literary fields. Novelists like H. G. Wells and Samuel Butler, playwrights like George Bernard Shaw, had kept up a steady polemical attack on the complacencies of the Victorian era. Georgian writing was another reflection of these trends.

4.2   Two men were principally responsible for initiating the 'movement', Rupert Brooke (1887–1915), and Edward Marsh (1872–1953). Brooke, already a poet of some reputation published his first volume, *Poems*, in 1911. Marsh was not a writer. A literary historian of the period described him in this way: 'In 1912, if he was known at all outside a very select circle, Edward Marsh was known as Winston Churchill's private secretary, an efficient, knowledgeable, and self-effacing Civil Servant who moved in the most rarified strata of titled and upper-class England.' (Ross *The Georgian Revolt*, p 102.) A wealthy man, he developed a collector's enthusiasm for contemporary painting, and then for poetry. He had known Brooke for several years, admired his *Poems*, and wrote an appreciative review in the spring of 1912. Later that year, believing that there were several good young poets who deserved a larger public, the two men decided to organize a selection of recent work, and in December 1912, *Georgian Poetry 1911-12* made its appearance, with Marsh as the editor. It met far greater success than either Brooke or Marsh expected, running to ten editions by May 1914, and by the end of 1919 selling thirteen thousand copies; while by the same date its successor *Georgian Poetry 1913-15*, published in 1915, had sold twelve thousand copies. Three further volumes appeared in 1917, 1919 and 1922. Marsh then felt that poetic taste had so changed that he was no longer the appropriate editor of such an anthology, and brought the project to an end.

THE ORIGINS OF GEORGIAN POETRY

4.3   The origins of Georgian poetry reveal a good deal about it. First, it was not really a 'movement', there was no manifesto, no thought-out literary programme, and no dominant poetic voice. It was an anthology assembled by a cultivated amateur of the arts, and as several critics have pointed out, it never lost its anthological character. Second, it was in part a marketing operation. The poets were already in print, however modestly. What the Georgian anthologies called into being was an audience. (There is distant analogy in our own day in the publishing successes of Penguin Books, who partly discovered and partly created an audience for a wide range of titles previously confined to expensive small editions for the specialist reader.) Changes in emphasis from volume to volume reflected Marsh's sense of what would best

Figure 5 Rupert Brooke by J. H. Thomas, 1930 (National Portrait Gallery)

please the mass of his readers. In his attitude to the range of other poetic experimentation of the period, Marsh was cautious, middle-of-the-road. He had an editor's, rather than a critic's, judgement, and while wanting to do the best for his poets, thought primarily in terms of readership. Third, the underlying ethos of the initial Georgian anthologies reflects the influence of Rupert Brooke, or at least of one aspect of his writing – its attempts at 'realism'. His own *Poems* had been attacked for this, for their 'unpleasantness', for his inclusion of 'ugly' aspects of experience. What this meant may be judged by a contemporary's remark:

> Everybody was talking about 'Channel Passage' and 'Menelaus and Helen':
> the younger people admired him for daring to write a sonnet about
> seasickness and to describe so cynically and realistically the old age of
> Helen and Menelaus, but, on the whole, even those who admired him were
> inclined to be shocked, many indeed were frankly annoyed at his bad taste
> and at the way in which, with arrogant undergraduate bravado, for so
> they considered it, he deliberately set out to flout long-cherished poetic
> conventions. (Cited in Ross *The Georgian Revolt*, p 114.)

'A Channel Passage', written in 1909, is a sonnet, comparing the pain of an unhappy love affair, with the pain of being seasick.

> The damned ship lurched and slithered. Quiet and quick
>   My cold gorge rose; the long sea rolled; I knew
> I must think hard of something, or be sick;
>   And could think hard of only one thing – *you!*
> You, you alone could hold my fancy ever!
>   And with you memories come, sharp pain, and dole.
> Now there's a choice – heartache or tortured liver!
>   A sea-sick body, or a you-sick soul!
>
> Do I forget you? Retchings twist and tie me,
>   Old meat, good meals, brown gobbets, up I throw.
> Do I remember? Acrid return and slimy,
>   The sobs and slobbers of a last year's woe.
> And still the sick ship rolls. 'Tis hard, I tell ye,
> To choose 'twixt love and nausea, heart and belly.

'Menelaus and Helen' is a pair of sonnets, the first describing in traditionally elevated style, Menelaus' moment of victorious reunion with Helen in Priam's ruined Troy. The second follows in ironic contrast:

> So far the poet. How should he behold
>   That journey home, the long connubial years?
>   He does not tell you how white Helen bears
> Child on legitimate child, becomes a scold,
> Haggard with virtue. Menelaus bold
>   Waxed garrulous, and sacked a hundred Troys
>   'Twixt noon and supper. And her golden voice
> Got shrill as he grew deafer. And both were old.
>
> Often he wonders why on earth he went
>   Troyward, or why poor Paris ever came.
>   Oft she weeps, gummy-eyed and impotent;
>   Her dry shanks twitch at Paris' mumbled name.
> So Menelaus nagged; and Helen cried;
> And Paris slept on by Scamander side.

The anti-romantic note probably strikes us today as uneasily assertive, an over-insistence pointing to something deeper than an attack on sentimental poetic conventions about love – Brooke's own failure to escape them with any completeness. Yet his defence of this side of his writing is revealing. Writing about another poem, he says:

> My own feeling is that to remove it would be to overbalance the book still
> more in the direction of unimportant prettiness. There's plenty of that sort
> of wash in the other pages for the readers who like it. They needn't read the
> parts that are new and serious. . . . I'm extra keen about the places where
> I think that thought and passion are, however clumsily, *not* so transmuted
> [into prettiness]. This was one of them. It seemed to have qualities of
> reality and novelty that made up for the clumsiness. . . . I should like it to
> stand, as a representative in the book of abortive poetry against literary
> verse. (Brooke *Collected Poems*, p lxx.)

Notice that Brooke's argument links 'literary verse' and 'prettiness' over against 'poetry' (even his own unsatisfactory attempts) and 'reality'. Perhaps there is something in the charge that 'A Channel Passage' and 'Menelaus' reflect an undergraduate impulse to shock. (You might like to compare them with another attack on genteel sentimental literary and social conventions – Yeats' 'On Those that Hated *The Playboy of the Western World*, 1907', written also in 1909, *Collected Poems*, p 124.) But in years when two such poems could be thought cynically realistic, a degree of over-emphasis is hardly surprising. As Brooke remarked of his critics 'True literary realism, they think, is a fearless reproduction of what real living men say when there is a clergyman in the room'. (p lxix.)

The mixed reaction to Brooke's poems contributed in an interesting way to the idea of the Georgian volumes. Recounting the origins of Georgian poetry in his Memoir prefacing Brooke's *Collected Poems*, Marsh recalls that one evening in the autumn of 1912 Brooke came out with a scheme to shock the contemporary reader into paying attention to recent poetry by writing poems in a variety of experimental styles, and publishing the results under various *noms de plume*, as a mock anthology. This would be, in effect, his reply to his more genteel and shockable reviewers. It was Marsh who modified this notion into a genuine anthology which would act as a showcase for good recent poets – Brooke amongst them. And Marsh seems also to have been responsible for altering the tone of the project. None of Brooke's 'unpleasant' poems were selected for *Georgian Poetry 1911-12*, and there was nothing experimental about any of the other material. 'Realism' of a kind is in evidence, but lacking Brooke's satirical energy. At the outset, the Georgian anthologies were born out of a spirit of accommodation with what Marsh felt the potential readership could stand.

REACTION AND CRITICISM

4.4   What did 'Georgian poetry' amount to? In his preface to the 1912 volume, Marsh hoped that the Georgian period would eventually rank with the 'several great poetic ages of the past', and sales apart, his anthologies made a considerable critical stir. As talented a poet as Wilfred Owen was elated to be 'held peer by the Georgians' (Press *A Map of Modern English Verse*, p 138). D. H. Lawrence, as we've seen (1.5), praised the first volume highly. Established literary opinion, a useful index of a different kind, took fright. In 1915, a reviewer complained that

> . . . a careful examination of these two volumes of Georgian poetry seems to suggest that during the last ten years or so English poetry has been approaching a condition of liberty and licence which threatens, not only to submerge old standards altogether, but, if persevered in to its logical limits, to hand over the sensitive art of verse to a general process of literary democratisation. (Cited in Stead *The New Poetic*, pp 61–2.)

Yet by 1920, 'Georgianism' was well on its way to becoming a term of critical contempt. The 1919 volume was slashingly reviewed for its 'corporate flavour of false simplicity', its failure to survive any 'test of reality',[5] and T. S. Eliot could refer, almost in passing, to 'the annual scourge of the Georgian anthology'.[6] Far from announcing a new age Georgian poetry came to be seen as the final spasm of the moribund nineteenth-century tradition, a thirdhand mixture of Wordsworth, Keats and Shelley, whose only valuable feature was the break with elements of Victorian writing – archaisms, literary pomposities, philosophic and religious moralizing, and the attitudinizing of the aesthetic 'Nineties.

> Georgian poetry was to be English but not aggressively imperialistic; pantheistic rather than atheistic; and simple as a child's reading book. These recommendations resulted in a poetry which could be praised *rather for what it was not than for what it was*. Eventually Georgianism became principally concerned with Nature and love and leisure and old age and childhood and animals and sleep and similar uncontroversial subjects. (Press *A Map of Modern English Verse*, p 119 (my italics).)

So Robert Graves and Laura Riding sardonically summed up the position in 1927, and for the next three decades the standard view held that Georgian poetry was technically slack, lacked ideas or individual feeling, and recommended an escape from twentieth-century reality into the pastoral fantasies of the London literary man weekending in the country.

Recent critics have, however, qualified this dismissal. C. K. Stead distinguishes between the early and later Georgian anthologies, arguing that though by 1922 Georgian writing was indeed regressive, the 1912 and 1915 volumes were different, and that Marsh was right in thinking his poets reflected a fresh feeling for life and a

[5] J. Middleton Murry *Aspects of Literature*, p 141.
[6] John Press *A Map of Modern English Verse*, p 82.

vigorous break with dead literary conventions. Stead maintains that these early Georgian anthologies began the task of creating a healthier poetic tradition, capable of expressing twentieth-century experience, though it took different and more powerful writers to complete it. In *The Georgian Revolt*, Ross argues similarly that in the pre-war years, there was a general poetic renewal, of which Georgianism was one expression, Imagism, together with other experimental trends, another, and of which the poetry of Eliot and Pound, whose influence eventually superannuated Georgian writing, happened simply to be the most powerful. He points out – and it is worth remembering – that there was no initial rivalry between Georgians and Imagists, that Pound nearly contributed to the 1912 volume, and that Eliot was not more critical of Georgian poetry than of other contemporary writing.

John Press argues on similar lines, and you can read his and Stead's view of the Georgians for yourself (*A Map of Modern English Verse*, pp 104–25; *The New Poetic*, pp 80–93). What none of these critics altogether faces however is the question of whether it is possible to take more than a literary historian's interest in Georgian poems. Do they still command enough of our attention *as poems* to justify the notion that here is a significant originating source of twentieth-century poetry? Or do we only read them as the museum exhibits of a defunct literary movement?

FOUR POEMS

4.5 ■ Look at this group of poems, and then make notes on these questions

a How much of the Graves/Riding comment on Georgian poetry applies to them – read the whole of it, not just the excerpt above (Press *A Map of Modern English Verse*, pp 118–19).

b Do any of them have qualities that are not mentioned in the comment? How would you judge their 'human' interest?

> *A Prospect of Death*
>
> If it should come to this,
> You cannot wake me with a kiss,
> Think I but sleep too late
> Or once again keep a cold angry state.
>
> So now you have been told—
> I or my breakfast may grow cold,
> But you must only say
> 'Why does he miss the best part of the day?'
>
> Even then you may be wrong;
> Through woods torn by a blackbird's song
> My thoughts may often roam
> While graver business makes me stay at home.
>
> There will be time enough
> To go back to the earth I love
> Some other day that week,
> Perhaps to find what all my life I seek.
>
> So do not dream of danger;
> Forgive my lateness or my anger;
> You have so much forgiven,
> Forgive me this or that, or Hell or Heaven.

Titmouse

If you would happy company win,
Dangle a palm-nut from a tree,
Idly in green to sway and spin,
Its now-pulped kernel for bait; and see,
   A nimble titmouse enter in.

Out of earth's vast unknown of air,
Out of all summer, from wave to wave,
He'll perch, and prank his feathers fair,
Jangle a glass-clear wildering stave,
   And take his commons there –

This tiny son of life; this spright,
By momentary Human sought,
Plume will his wing in the dappling light,
Clash timbrel shrill and gay –
And into time's enormous nought,
   Sweet-fed, will flit away.

wildering = bewildering
take his commons = have his meal

The Snare

I hear a sudden cry of pain!
   There is a rabbit in a snare:
Now I hear the cry again,
   But I cannot tell from where.

But I cannot tell from where
   He is calling out for aid;
Crying on the frightened air,
   Making everything afraid.

Making everything afraid,
   Wrinkling up his little face,
As he cries again for aid;
   And I cannot find the place!

And I cannot find the place
   Where his paw is in the snare:
Little one! Oh, little one!
   I am searching everywhere.

October

The green elm with the one great bough of gold
Lets leaves into the grass slip, one by one, –
The short hill grass, the mushrooms small, milk-white,
Harebell and scabious and tormentil,
That blackberry and gorse, in dew and sun,
Bow down to; and the wind travels too light
To shake the fallen birch leaves from the fern;
The gossamers wander at their own will,
At heavier steps than birds' the squirrels scold.
The rich scene has grown fresh again and new
As Spring and to the touch is not more cool

35

CHRIST'S COLLEGE
LIBRARY

Than it is warm to the gaze; and now I might
As happy be as earth is beautiful,
Were I some other or with earth could turn
In alternation of violet and rose,
Harebell and snowdrop, at their season due,
And gorse that has no time not to be gay.
But if this be not happiness, – who knows?
Some day I shall think this a happy day,
And this mood by the name of melancholy
Shall no more blackened and obscured be.

Discussion

4.6   a   The main points in the Graves/Riding paragraph apply, I would think, to all four poems: straightforward language, no heavy Victorian moralizing, concern with Nature and the subjects of old age, love and animals.

b   For 'human' interest, I would put first 'A Prospect of Death', then 'October', then 'The Snare', and lastly 'Titmouse'. Moreover, the two former poems seem to me to have qualities not expressed in the Graves/Riding criticism. Perhaps they are not controversial, but neither are they as tame and colourless as that comment (more a gibe than a criticism?) certainly implies. Both convey an individual experience of some complexity and force.■

'October' begins straightforwardly enough, with its delicate and precise evocation of a particular moment in the year – the sights and sounds of quiet natural activity – the falling leaves, the light wind, the scolding squirrels – but the writer's feelings about this scene are far from simple. Is he enjoying or is he not? And if not, why is he unable to enjoy it simply? Is he only expressing a personal moodiness? What does he mean by 'Were I some other or with earth could turn . . .'? Is he critical of his odd reaction? Does the end of the poem mean that to remember the day as 'happy' would falsify the more elusive and complicated truth? Or that its happiness *is* the truth, and its melancholy false and superficial? Or does it mean that 'the name of melancholy' is too crude a description of the actual experience, which includes both direct happiness in the scene, and the opposing truth that however much he might want to no human being *can* live simply, in the moment, like plants and animals? These questions are raised, not answered, but they – not Nature – are what the poem is about.

'Titmouse', in contrast, has minimal 'human' interest. Perhaps it's not unsuccessful in conveying the writer's tenderness about the bird. But what else is there? The thought in the last verse? I'm not convinced by it. In 'October', the ideas grow directly out of the writer's experience, as he presents it in the poem, and its tone of tentative self-questioning is appropriate. But with 'Titmouse', it seems to me that his reflection has not been 'lived'. It seems tacked on to the experience, developed for the sake of the poem, and hence portentous in tone, and even commonplace. (To be literal, for a moment, a well-fed bird *does not* fly off into 'time's enormous nought'. Nor did this writer: he wrote his poem.) It is a poem I would prefer if it had stuck to observation, and it is 'uncontroversial' in exactly the way Graves and Riding accused Georgian poetry of being.

What about 'The Snare'? I think this poem is trying – and failing – to do something difficult: write about a spontaneous impulse, that most people can immediately share, without saying anything more about it. The poet offers no 'thought', no new insight into the experience. Simply, he tries to convey how he felt. Does it fail because it goes on too long? Is its evocation of the creature's situation not vivid enough? Is it too insistent? The repetition of the last line of one verse as the first line of the next is, presumably, meant to convey intensity, yet the effect is rather to thin out the impact across four stanzas. Is the problem its explicitness? Or the mechanical effect of the rhythm? I think it is the kind of poem to keep in mind as a warning about overdoing simplicity of language.

I paired 'A Prospect of Death' with 'October' because both poems have qualities not reflected in the Graves/Riding comment, but 'A Prospect' also differs from the rest in being about a human relationship, and not just the writer and his feelings about Nature. One point about the language is worth noticing: though simple enough, it is full of implication, even mystery. 'Keep a cold angry state' – to 'keep state' is a dignified, public thing to do, and this suggests public ceremonies for death, as well as a certain kind of living mood, a self-dramatizing hard-edged anger. 'Graver business' – the pun on 'grave' again raises the idea of death, as does the double sense of 'To go back to the earth I love'. What about 'to find what all my life I seek'? Does this mean he is seeking death, or 'Hell or Heaven', all his life, as well as something in the natural world? Both presumably. These implied meanings are necessary to the basic idea of the poem which is to say that his final absence in death will resemble different kinds of withdrawal in life – into anger, the love of nature, work, thoughts about the after-life – and yet also to recognize that to say this is not more than a loving evasion of the truth, that death is an absence of an entirely different kind. 'Death', as William Empson has remarked, 'is the trigger of the literary man's biggest gun', and perhaps it's unfair to the other poems to group them with 'A Prospect of Death'. But it's a reminder that uncontroversial poems about old age, and the love of nature, are not necessarily slight in meaning, or lacking either in human content, or in the impressive skill with which this poet can suggest so much more than he states.

4.7   Some further comments on the poems by colleagues in the course team.

Several liked 'October' much less than I did. One thought it less good than 'The Snare'. Another remarked: 'I don't think this poem is either delicate, precise, or successful.' Another asked: 'Has the poet really conveyed any very definite mood so that one feels a need to interpret it? The fancies about the wind "travelling light" and the gorse "bowing down" to the grass don't seem much more than sentimental to me.'

Another commented of 'Titmouse': 'Birds do not sing while they take their commons. That would attract other birds to the spot, and our feathered friend would be forced to abandon his nourishing coconut. More generally, it lacks a sense of proportion which is typical of Georgian poetry of the worst kind. It wants to be about something that is small yet life-enriching, but it can't resist a bid for profundity as well.'

Another added this remark about 'The Snare': 'The repetition is presumably meant to convey, and to me succeeds in doing so, not simply intensity but a particular movement, the poet's head turning this way and that as the cries come again and he doesn't know where to look for them; a similar movement in the trapped animal is not far out of the picture. It's surely the line "Little one! Oh little one!" that, if anything, sinks this poem. The simplicity of the rest of the language seems wholly appropriate. But "little one" suddenly offers a "thought". A sententious human endearment, as to a ruffed and velvet-knickerbockered child, suddenly intrudes. I prefer the reflex to the meditative reaction. (And so, one imagines, would the rabbit.)'

The authors of these poems are: James Stephens 'The Snare', Edward Thomas 'October', Walter de la Mare 'Titmouse', Andrew Young 'A Prospect of Death'. Stephens' poem appeared in *Georgian Poetry 1913-15* (1915), Thomas' in *Last Poems* (1918), de la Mare's in *Georgian Poetry 1920-22* (1922), and Young's in *The Green Man* (1947).

4.8   I chose 'The Snare' and 'Titmouse' to illustrate the weakness of the characteristic Georgian poem; and 'October' and 'A Prospect of Death' to show that the Georgian formula needn't *necessarily* lead to poems meriting the Graves/Riding dismissal. Edward Thomas (1878–1917) did not appear in any of the Georgian volumes, though other contributors tried to persuade Marsh to include him. (One wrote: '. . . it would be splendid if the next Georgian book included any other new poetry of comparable individuality and power.' (Ross, p 177.) As indeed it would have been.) Andrew Young (1885–1973) published his first collection in 1910. Nor did he appear in Marsh's anthologies. Most critics today, however, would think of Thomas and Young as Georgian poets. (See Press, pp 114–16.) James Reeves, for example, includes them both in his Penguin *Georgian Poetry* (1962) which he chose on the principle of including only poems 'worthy of the attention of the contemporary reader' (p xx). Perhaps then there is an answer to the critical dismissal of the Georgian writers other than that of the literary historian, and that is not to identify Georgian poetry wholly with the poets of the original Georgian anthologies.

REALISM AND GEORGIAN POETRY

4.9 But we still have to look at the positive claim for early Georgian poems, and Ross's claim that they expressed a new 'realism', already a feature of the novels of the period, is a useful formula for this. You might begin by thinking that 'realism' is an odd term to use of poetry, and in its confined sense, as a description for a certain kind of novel, you would be right. More troublingly, 'realism' is a complex idea in its application to literature. (If you took A302 *The Nineteenth-century Novel*[7], perhaps you will remember just how complex.) In one sense, we habitually contrast 'the real' with the 'imaginary', yet in another we praise a writer's 'imaginative vision' for its superior grasp of 'reality'. Still in the simpler sense, poetry has been often committed to conveying an 'imaginary' world. As the Renaissance critic and poet, Sir Philip Sidney put it, '[Nature's] world is brazen, the Poets only deliver a golden [one]' and it's a notion strongly re-emphasized in the Romantic period where imagination is the key term for the discussion of poetry. During the nineteenth century, certainly, the growing prestige of the novel exerted a pressure on poets. Narrative poetry flourished, though significantly based on romances and legends like the Arthurian cycle reworked by Tennyson. Poems exploring the recesses of individual character opened up another vein, though again direct competition with the novel was often avoided by choosing figures from the past, as in Browning's studies of Renaissance artists and priests.

But it is not in that sense of imitating some formal traits of the novel that poetry involves 'realism'. Think, for a moment, of the way each generation of human beings senses life freshly, both negatively as a reaction against the authority of the past (in the form of parents, teachers, policemen, public moralists, etc.); and positively, in its immediate experience of the fact that change seems essential to organized human life. Writers react similarly against their admired predecessors. They look for other ways to define 'reality', new forms of language to express the new shapes in which human experience comes to them. In that sense, there is a perpetual duty on all writers to be 'realistic', and poets no less than novelists ignore it at their peril. Yet nothing is easier than to ignore it. The past has immense authority over our ways of valuing and living. The greater the writer, the more difficult he is to challenge. That is what Eliot means when he writes about the lesser eighteenth-century poets:

> What really happened is that after Pope there was no one who thought and felt nearly enough like Pope to be able to use his language quite successfully; but a good many second-rate writers tried to write something like it, unaware of the fact that the change of sensibility demanded a change of idiom.

[7] The Open University (1973) A302 *The Nineteenth-century Novel and Its Legacy*, The Open University Press.

Sensibility alters from generation to generation in everybody, whether we will or no; but expression is only altered by a man of genius. (Eliot *Selected Prose*, pp 163-4.)

In speaking of the 'realism' of poetry, we should think in terms of 'sensibility', of human consciousness, of the ways in which we respond to the world and to each other, the ways in which we define what is worth talking about, the ways in which we judge and evaluate. This kind of 'realism' is one way of describing Brooke's 'unpleasant' poems (4.3), which discuss love in what was then an aggressively new manner. Brooke was saying, if you like, 'past literature has taught us an untrue account of the feelings: love and seasickness don't happen in separate compartments, one publishable in traditional sonnet form, the other not, but to the same whole individual human being; and contrary to tradition in these matters, it's ridiculous to think that Menelaus and Helen didn't get old, and like every other married couple, fall away from the high romance which literature has made out of Homer's story.' The 'realism' of poetry lies in the assertion that such-and-such a received attitude towards experience is limited, shallow, onesided, even untrue; that the experience is like *this*; that there is *this* side of it never properly understood before; that the experience is more complex, or simpler, or more – or less – valuable than people have been led to accept. This is the spirit in which Lawrence welcomed the first Georgian anthology for displaying an optimistic and zestful interest in life instead of the nightmarish *unreality* (as Lawrence felt) of Ibsen's and Hardy's pessimism. Such 'realism' is of course, necessarily relative, conditioned by the history it challenges, vulnerable in its turn to the successful denunciation of later 'realisms'. In a minor degree, the 'realism' of the Georgian anthologies is of this kind.

4.10   Here is a straightforward example.

> *The Bird of Paradise*
> Here comes Kate Summers, who, for gold,
>   Takes any man to bed:
> 'You knew my friend, Nell Barnes,' she said;
>   'You knew Nell Barnes – she's dead.
>
> 'Nell Barnes was bad on all you men,
>   Unclean, a thief as well;
> Yet all my life I have not found
>   A better friend than Nell.
>
> 'So I sat at her side at last,
>   For hours till she was dead;
> And yet she had no sense at all
>   Of any word I said.
>
> 'For all her cry but came to this –
>   "Not for the world! Take care:
> Don't touch that bird of paradise,
>   Perched on the bed-post there!"
>
> 'I asked her would she like some grapes,
>   Some damsons ripe and sweet;
> A custard made with new-laid eggs,
>   Or tender fowl to eat.
>
> 'I promised I would follow her,
>   To see her in her grave;
> And buy a wreath with borrowed pence,
>   If nothing I could save.

CHRIST'S COLLEGE
LIBRARY

'Yet still her cry but came to this –
    "Not for the world! Take care:
Don't touch that bird of paradise,
    Perched on the bed-post there!" '

This poem by W. H. Davies, printed in the 1915 volume, was condemned by a reviewer as a piece of 'sheer ugliness', presumably because it is about two prostitutes, one with veneral disease. Yet it is only a modern example of what Wordsworth had long ago practised in *Lyrical Ballads*, a poem inviting the reader to recognize an actual human being, without special pleading or extraneous moral and social judgements.

The same reviewer described the author of the following poem as displaying 'a degree of self-abandonment which is so invertebrate as to be practically abnormal'. (Cited in Stead *The New Poetic*, p 62.) It is too long to print in full, but this extract gives the flavour.

Snap-Dragon

'I like to see,' she said, and she crouched her down,
She sunk into my sight like a settling bird;
And her bosom couched in the confines of her gown
Like heavy birds at rest there, softly stirred
By her measured breaths: 'I like to see,' said she,
'The snap dragon put out his tongue at me.'

She laughed, she reached her hand out to the flower
Closing its crimson throat: my own throat in her power
Strangled, my heart swelled up so full
As it would burst its wineskin in my throat,
Choke me in my own crimson; I watched her pull
The gorge of the gaping flower, till the blood did float

        Over my eyes and I was blind –
Her large brown hand stretched over
The windows of my mind,
And in the dark I did discover
Things I was out to find:

(seven lines omitted)

Then suddenly she looked up
And I was blind in a tawny-gold day
Till she took her eyes away.

So she came down from above
And emptied my heart of love . . .
So I held my heart aloft
To the cuckoo that fluttered above,
And she settled soft.

This, by D. H. Lawrence, appeared in the 1912 volume. It is an uneven poem, but the fresh – and as we have come to think of it – Lawrentian, intensity of feeling is still striking, and clearly the source of that disgusted accusation of 'self-abandonment'.

■ Before leaving this extract, make a note on another charge against Georgian poetry: that it was technically incompetent. The reviewer quoted in 4.4, for example, wrote about 'a condition of liberty and licence'. Do you see anything in these lines to account for such a view? What do you think yourself of the writing?

Here's a third example of the 'realistic' strain from the 1912 anthology:

Miss Loo

When thin-strewn memory I look through,
I see most clearly poor Miss Loo,
Her tabby cat, her cage of birds,
Her nose, her hair – her muffled words,
And how she'd open her green eyes,
As if in some immense surprise,
Whenever as we sat at tea,
She made some small remark to me.

It's always drowsy summer when
From out the past she comes again;
The westering sunshine in a pool
Floats in her parlour still and cool;
While the slim bird its lean wires shakes,
As into piercing song it breaks;
Till Peter's pale-green eyes ajar
Dream, wake; wake, dream, in one brief bar;
And I am sitting, dull and shy,
And she with gaze of vacancy,
And large hands folded on the tray,
Musing the afternoon away;
Her satin bosom heaving slow
With sighs that softly ebb and flow,
And her plain face in such dismay,
It seems unkind to look her way:
Until all cheerful back will come
Her cheerful gleaming spirit home;
And one would think that poor Miss Loo
Asked nothing else, if she had you.

Triviality is another charge levelled at Georgian writing. Would it be a fair comment on this poem by Walter de la Mare?

In reading the next poem, consider two points:

a   the connection between the origins of Georgian poetry and the spirit of humanitarian reform associated with Liberal politics of the Edwardian period;

b   its 'technical' competence.

Geraniums

Stuck in a bottle on the window-sill,
In the cold gaslight burning gaily red
Against the luminous blue of starless London night
These flowers are mine: while somewhere out of sight
In some black-throated alley's stench and heat,
Oblivious of the racket of the street,
A poor old weary woman lies in bed.

Broken with lust and drink, blear-eyed and ill,
Her battered bonnet nodding on her head,
From a dark arch she clutched my sleeve and said:
'I've sold no bunch today, nor touched a bite . . .
Son, buy six-pennorth; and 'twill mean a bed.'

So blazing gaily red
Against the luminous deeps
Of starless London night
They burn for my delight:
While somewhere, snug in bed,
A worn old woman sleeps.

And yet tomorrow will these blooms be dead
With all their lively beauty; and tomorrow
May end the light lusts and the heavy sorrow
Of that old body with the nodding head,
The last oath muttered, the last pint drained deep,
She'll sink, as Cleopatra sank, to sleep;
Nor need to barter blossoms for a bed.

This poem is by Wilfred W. Gibson, and appeared in the 1912 anthology.

Discussion

4.11 The Lawrence extract is, on the whole, successful but it is also loosely written. The way the second verse spills over into the next is surely careless; and the third verse would benefit from cutting. The rhymes often seem heavy going, as if the poet felt a duty to find them, but had little enthusiasm. On the other hand, the sensuous power of the first and second verses is remarkable. It is an early poem, written before Lawrence had worked free from the influence of rhymed and stanza-ed verse. (You could compare it with 'All Souls' (2.13).) The form fits the feeling badly, and suggests a writer struggling to accommodate his own 'meaning' to the demands of an unhelpful model of regular rhymed verse.

'Miss Loo' is trivial only if you insist that all poems should have a large, general, profound subject. I find it altogether successful in capturing Miss Loo's quality with affection and humour, and explaining why her memory is now vivid and attractive. But one can see how easily such poems can slip into arch and cosy complacency.

'Geraniums' has a direct 'social' quality that illustrates the connection with Liberal reform, but notice how little the poet's sympathy actually bridges the gap between him and the old woman. He tries, most conscientiously, to 'connect' with her condition, but a phrase like 'broken with lust and drink' reduces her to the level of a pitiable *object*. It is his feeling for the flowers that comes across most strongly. Technically, the poet is not incompetent. Look at the rhymes: the poet has managed to sustain similar, if not identical rhymes throughout, which helps it attain unity of effect. But the strain begins to show in the last verse (notice especially 'tomorrow/sorrow') and elsewhere the language is diffuse and approaches cliché: 'poor old weary woman', 'battered bonnet', 'worn old woman'. The reference to Cleopatra, too, seems dragged in. The general style of the poem is direct, un-formal, and a major literary allusion comes as a surprise. It's a heavy-handed way of making sure that we think well of the old creature ('broken with lust' etc.). I doubt whether this poem supports charges of technical incompetence, but it does not seem to me *accomplished* writing. It lacks the keen artistic discipline that makes sure that the words all count, and that they are the right words, and there is not the compensatory inner force of the Lawrence poem. ■

4.12 Georgian 'realism' had another result represented in these excerpts from the 1918 volume.

The Assault

The beating of the guns grows louder.
'*Not long, boys, now.*'
My heart burns whiter, fearfuller, prouder.
Hurricanes grow
As guns redouble their fire.
Through the shaken periscope peeping,
I glimpse their wire:
Black earth, fountains of earth rise, leaping,
Spouting like shocks of meeting waves,
Death's fountains are playing,
Shells like shrieking birds rush over;
Crash and din rises higher.
A stream of lead raves
Over us from the left . . . (we safe under cover!)
Crash! Reverberation! Crash!
Acrid smoke billowing. Flash upon flash.
Black smoke drifting. The German line
Vanishes in confusion, smoke. Cries, and cry
Of our men, '*Gah, yer swine!*
Ye're for it,' die
In a hurricane of shell.

One cry:
'*We're coming soon! look out!*'
There is opened hell
Over there; fragments fly,
Rifles and bits of men whirled at the sky:
Dust, smoke, thunder! A sudden bout
Of machine guns chattering . . .
And redoubled battering,
As if in fury at their daring! . . .

No good staring.

Time soon now . . . home . . . house on a sunny hill . . .
Gone like a flickered page!
Time soon now . . . zero . . . will engage . . .

(82 more lines omitted)

Figure 6   Robert M. B. Nichols by A. E. John, 1921 (National Portrait Gallery)

'*In the Pink*'

So Davies wrote: 'This leaves me in the pink.'
Then scrawled his name: 'Your loving sweetheart, Willie'
With crosses for a hug. He'd had a drink
Of rum and tea; and, though the barn was chilly,
For once his blood ran warm; he had pay to spend.
Winter was passing; soon the year would mend.

He couldn't sleep that night. Stiff in the dark
He groaned and thought of Sundays at the farm,
When he'd go out as cheerful as a lark
In his best suit to wander arm-in-arm
With brown-eyed Gwen, and whisper in her ear
The simple, silly things she liked to hear.

And then he thought: tomorrow night we trudge
Up to the trenches, and my boots are rotten.
Five miles of stodgy clay and freezing sludge,
And everything but the wretchedness forgotten.
Tonight he's in the pink; but soon he'll die.
And still the war goes on; *he* don't know why.

It's a Queer Time

It's hard to know if you're alive or dead
When steel and fire go roaring through your head.

One moment you'll be crouching at your gun
Traversing, mowing heaps down half in fun;
The next, you choke and clutch at your right breast –
No time to think – leave all – and off you go . . .
To Treasure Island where the Spice winds blow,
To lovely groves of mango, quince and lime –
Breathe no goodbye, but ho, for the Red West!
    It's a queer time.

(1 verse omitted)

Or you'll be dozing safe in your dug-out –
A great roar – the trench shakes and falls about –
You're struggling, gasping, struggling, then . . . hullo!
Elsie comes tripping gaily down the trench,
Hanky to nose – that lyddite makes a stench –
Getting her pinafore all over grime.
Funny! because she died ten years ago!
    It's a queer time.

The trouble is, things happen much too quick;
Up jumps the Bosches, rifles thump and click,
You stagger, and the whole scene fades away:
Even good Christians don't like passing straight
From Tipperary or their Hymn of Hate
To Allelujiah-chanting, and the chime
Of golden harps . . . and . . . I'm not well today . . .
    It's a queer time.

lyddite = gunpowder

The authors of these poems are, respectively, Robert Nichols (1893–1944), Siegfried
Sassoon (1886–1967), and Robert Graves (b. 1895).

4.13 To us, these or similar direct accounts of trench warfare have become familiar, but to
appreciate their original impact, it is only necessary to turn to several other poems
in the Georgian anthologies which express, though in a muted way, the standard
patriotic and heroic rhetoric about the war. The 1915 volume included 'The Soldier',

Brooke's well-known sonnet epitomizing a romantic patriotism about the war which was later demolished by poets like Sassoon and Wilfred Owen (discussed in Units 4–5). The 1918 volume printed, along with the poems quoted above, John Freeman's 'Happy is England Now' ('. . . happiest is England now/In those that fight, and watch with pride and tears'), Maurice Baring's 'In Memoriam, A. H.,' an elegy on the heroism of a friend killed in the battle, and the following by Herbert Asquith.

The Volunteer

Here lies the clerk who half his life had spent
Toiling at ledgers in a city grey,
Thinking that so his days would drift away
With no lance broken in life's tournament:
Yet ever 'twixt the books and his bright eyes
The gleaming eagles of the legions came,
And horsemen, charging under phantom skies,
Went thundering past beneath the oriflamme.

And now those waiting dreams are satisfied;
From twilight to the halls of dawn he went;
His lance is broken; but he lies content
With that high hour, in which he lived and died.
And falling thus, he wants no recompense,
Who found his battle in the last resort;
Nor needs he any hearse to bear him hence,
Who goes to join the men of Agincourt.

oriflamme = battle standard

■ Make brief notes on the differences between this poem and 'In the Pink'. Is 'realism' a useful idea in comparing them? Remember that I have suggested we should use the term 'realism' to cover attitudes, judgements, the new consciousness the poet wants us to share, and not just accurate observation.

4.14 Taking the three poems about trench warfare together would you say they were anti-war in spirit? Do you see any common ground between them and the following extract from a poem by W. W. Gibson in the 1915 Georgian anthology?

The Gorse

In dream, again within the clean, cold hell
Of glazed and aching silence he was trapped;
And, closing in, the blank walls of his cell
Crushed stifling on him . . . when the bracken snapped,
Caught in his clutching fingers; and he lay
Awake upon his back among the fern,
With free eyes travelling the wide blue day,
Unhindered, unremembering; while a burn
Tinkled and gurgled somewhere out of sight,
Unheard of him; till suddenly aware
Of its cold music, shivering in the light,
He raised himself, and with far-ranging stare
Looked all about him; and with dazed eyes wide
Saw, still as in a numb, unreal dream,

Black figures scouring a far hillside,
With now and then a sunlit rifle's gleam;
And knew the hunt was hot upon his track:
Yet hardly seemed to mind, somehow, just then . . .
But kept on wondering why they looked so black
On that hot hillside, all those little men
Who scurried round like beetles – twelve, all told . . .
He counted them twice over; and began
A third time reckoning them, and could not hold
His starved wits to the business, while they ran
So brokenly, and always stuck at 'five' . . .
And 'One, two, three, four, five,' a dozen times
He muttered . . . 'Can you catch a fish alive?'
Sang mocking echoes of old nursery rhymes
Through the strained, tingling hollow of his head.

(26 lines omitted)

The subject is not the war, by the way, but a convict on the run.

Discussion

4.15   a   I think the main differences between 'In the Pink' and 'The Volunteer' are these. First, the language: Sassoon's poem uses either Davies' own words, or a flat 'prosaic' reporting style ('He couldn't sleep that night' etc.) which keeps close to Davies' actual experience; whereas Asquith tends to inflate and decorate, or use vague metaphors that disguise ('From twilight to the halls of dawn he went' means 'he died'), or misrepresent ('his lance is broken' – to what actual situation in the war does that apply?) Second, each poem is competently written in its way, but Sassoon's is more subtle; it plays off the formal aspect of rhyme, rhythm and stanza against the flat un-'poetic' language to get a deflating effect, which produces the satirical bite of that last '*he don't know why*'. The feeling varies between a helpless sympathy for Davies, a refusal to idealize him, and a certain grim insistence on truth to fact. Asquith is monotonous, using the poetic form to elevate, as a kind of oratory, wholly confident that *he* can speak for the volunteer ('he wants no recompense'), intrinsically patronizing. Third, Asquith's poem works as a disguised political operation that not only assimilates the clerk into a certain view of the national destiny (Agincourt as a symbol of English military supremacy over Continental powers), but makes that seem life's profoundly satisfying goal; Sassoon's is slightly political in its conclusion, *but openly so*; and mainly it's concerned to convey a kind of experience, not to persuade you to join somebody's side.

As to 'realism', the term is obviously useful both in the narrow sense of 'factually truthful', and in the more extended meaning I have been suggesting. Asquith's poem not only evades the clerk's actual experience, it makes the reader complicit in a false consciousness about it. Sassoon's poem tries to ask a question, to use Davies' actual experience as a test of attitudes, of values. Davies 'don't know why' the war goes on – despite (so the implication runs) what gets said in public about such men. Does the reader?

I should add that some course team members thought Sassoon's poem patronizing as well. One remarked: 'Has he any imagination of the true Davies? Surely he totally fails to get inside Davies' mind, and that's the fact that really interests us. Davies' thoughts, as reported by Sassoon, are very stupid, self-pitying, and uninteresting. But in fact, they're not Davies' thoughts at all: they are just Sassoon being sorry for him.'

b   Of the three poems about trench warfare, only Sassoon's shows explicit anti-war sentiment, and that of a mild kind. Nichols' poem perhaps implies it, but mainly conveys a direct experience of assault – the sensations and feelings, the suppressed hysteria, the noise and stress, and so forth. Graves' poem has a satirical flavour, but mainly shows what it feels like to be suddenly wounded. Like Sassoon, and more subtly I think, Graves uses a plain, colloquial style, as of an officer speaking to a friend in the average language of his type and time, but suggests how inadequate such language is to the experience he's actually having. (Notice the end, especially.) 'It's a queer time' becomes, in its understatement and stoic reserve, an ironic refrain. What have these poems in common with the extract from 'The Gorse'? Gibson also works in a plain style, exploring an experience a bit like Graves' with its interplay of reality and dream. But the point I'd stress is that he is recording an *individual experience as vividly as he can*. As, more autobiographically, are Nichols, Sassoon and Graves. This is a major virtue of Georgian 'realism', present also in the poems by Davies, and de la Mare – though of course the experiences they were conveying were very different – and it marks off the best Georgian poems from the kind that gave the movement such a bad reputation. ◼

4.16   ◼   Here is one more pair to try this criterion on. Which of the following do you feel expresses a fresh sense of individual experience?

Full Moon

One night as Dick lay half asleep
    Into his drowsy eyes
A great still light began to creep
    From out the silent skies.
It was the lovely moon's, for when
    He raised his dreamy head,
Her surge of silver filled the pane
    And streamed across his bed.
So, for awhile, each gazed at each –
    Dick and the solemn moon –
Till, climbing slowly on her way,
    She vanished, and was gone.

'*It was the lovely moon*'

It was the lovely moon – she lifted
Slowly her white brow among
Bronze cloud-waves that ebbed and drifted
Faintly, faintlier afar.
Calm she looked, yet pale with wonder,
Sweet in unwonted thoughtfulness,
Watching the earth that dwindled under
Faintly, faintlier afar.
It was the lovely moon that lovelike
Hovered over the wandering, tired
Earth, her bosom grey and dovelike,
Hovering beautiful as a dove . . .
The lovely moon: – her soft light falling
Lightly on roof and poplar and pine –
Tree to tree whispering and calling,
Wonderfully in the silvery shine
Of the round, lovely, thoughtful moon.

Ezra Pound once wrote, expressing a cardinal idea of Imagist writing:

> Say what you will in two
> Words, and get thru,
> Long frilly
> Palaver is silly.

On that basis which of these poems would he have preferred?

Discussion

4.17 'Full Moon' by Walter de la Mare appeared in the 1915 volume; 'It was the lovely moon' by John Freeman in the 1918 volume. Despite its 'dreamy' atmosphere, the first is surely in the early Georgian vein – it directly conveys an experience – but not the second. Freeman's borrowing from the de la Mare (in the title and opening line) illustrates the tendency of Georgian poets to in-breed – a fact which tells a good deal about Marsh's critical limitations as an editor, and supports the later accusation that Georgian poets wrote to a formula. Notice both how much more adjectival Freeman's poem is, and how vague are its metaphors. The moon has a brow and eyes in lines 1–7, while verbs like 'look' and 'watch' suggest the human; but in line 12, it has become a dove; then in line 17 ('thoughtful') reverts to the human. (Of the last line, a colleague notes: 'This strange lady has nothing between her eyebrows and her bosom. What, therefore, does she think with?') Contrast de la Mare's '*solemn* moon' (line 10) to describe the effect of the half-awake boy and the moon looking at each other.

I imagine that Pound would have preferred de la Mare. Both Imagist principles and Pound's interest in them will be directly discussed in Units 4–5. You can find out now about the Imagist movement in John Press, *A Map of Modern English Verse*, pp 30–46. ∎

RUDYARD KIPLING – 'PUBLIC' POETRY

4.18 We have seen that early Georgian poetry shared in a reaction against some late Victorian assumptions about poetic language and subject matter. C. K. Stead further argues that it liberated poetic taste from the social and political influence exerted by a dominantly conservative 'poetry of political retrenchment, committed to conserve political and social ideas and institutions doomed to collapse' (*The New Poetic*, p 69) expressed by writers like Sir Henry Newbolt (1862–1938), Alfred Austin (see 3.2), and above all, Rudyard Kipling (1865–1936). You should read Stead's argument for yourself. He quotes poems by Newbolt and Austin which make an enlightening contrast with the Georgian poems we have been discussing. I want here to look at a poem of Kipling's partly because he is one of the few poets of the century who achieved something like 'popular' reputation, who spoke to and for readers outside the usual audience for poetry, and partly to raise a point about poetic language.

> *The White Man's Burden*
> 1899
>
> (The United States and the Philippine Islands)
>
> Take up the White Man's burden –
>   Send forth the best ye breed –
> Go bind your sons to exile
>   To serve your captives' need;

To wait in heavy harness
    On fluttered folk and wild –
Your new-caught, sullen peoples,
    Half devil and half child.

Take up the White Man's burden –
    In patience to abide,
To veil the threat of terror
    And check the show of pride;
By open speech and simple,
    An hundred times made plain,
To seek another's profit,
    And work another's gain.

Take up the White Man's burden –
    The savage wars of peace –
Fill full the mouth of Famine
    And bid the sickness cease;
And when your goal is nearest
    The end for others sought,
Watch Sloth and heathen Folly
    Bring all your hope to nought.

Figure 7   Rudyard Kipling by W. Strang, 1927
(National Portrait Gallery)

Take up the White Man's burden –
    No tawdry rule of kings,
But toil of serf and sweeper –
    The tale of common things.
The ports ye shall not enter,
    The roads ye shall not tread,
Go make them with your living,
    And mark them with your dead!

Take up the White Man's burden –
    And reap his old reward:
The blame of those ye better,
    The hate of those ye guard –
The cry of hosts ye humour
    (Ah, slowly!) toward the light: –
'Why brought ye us from bondage,
    Our loved Egyptian night?'

Take up the White Man's burden –
    Ye dare not stoop to less –
Nor call too loud on Freedom
    To cloak your weariness
By all ye cry or whisper,
    By all ye leave or do,
The silent sullen peoples
    Shall weigh your Gods and you.

Take up the White Man's Burden –
    Have done with childish days –
The lightly proferred laurel,
    The easy, ungrudged praise.
Comes now, to search your manhood
    Through all the thankless years,
Cold-edged with dear-bought wisdom.
    The judgement of your peers!

The sub-title explains the poem's occasion: when the United States took over the Philippine Islands.

■ How does this poem differ from the kind we have been looking at in subject matter, and in language? How would you describe its tone of voice? What do you think it said to the British reader, as distinct from the American? Two details to consider: what is the effect of Kipling's use of 'ye'; and of the allusion to Moses leading the Israelites out of Egypt into the Promised Land (fifth verse)?

Discussion

4.19 This is a public poem, occasioned by a public event. Kipling undertakes to speak not for himself, but for the builders of the British Empire, even for the White Man, the European imperialist as the bringer of order and enlightenment to the rest of the world. Its language is, at least on the surface, plain and direct, immediately understandable, with some memorably compact phrases ('the savage wars of peace', 'tawdry rule of kings'); the verse form is straightforward, the rhythms regular and emphatic. The tone of voice is confident, stern, imperative (look at the tenses of the verbs). 'Ye' is, I think, taken from biblical usage to lend impersonal dignity and resonance. Perhaps the hymn-like stanza form contributes the same effect. The reference to Moses and the Israelites fits in to this pattern. Yet if we look at it more closely, it reveals what is I think a general characteristic of the poem – repeated distortions of the reality it appeals to. Moses was an Israelite, sharing the language, culture and race of the people he led from bondage. Was that the situation of the imperialist? Evidently not. Kipling uses the allusion to dignify the situation of the imperialist administrator struggling with the obdurate resistance of subject peoples, but in doing so, he falsifies it. Again, if we look at the first verse, the implication is that the 'heavy harness' of imperial rule weighed more painfully on the shoulders of the soldier or district commissioner than on that of the 'fluttered folk' he ruled. At the very least, that seems a simplification. In the fourth verse, the White Man's burden is:

> No tawdry rule of kings
> But toil of serf and sweeper –
> The tale of common things.

Here the distortion of reality is more striking. The imperialist functionary may be called a servant in the sense that he obeys a political hierarchy, and a professional code, but was his work as unrewarding and unprestigious as that of serfs and sweepers? It seems improbable. Surely, the manner of the poem evades – where it doesn't actually misrepresent – the actualities it deals with. This, it seems to me, is the key to what the poem says, or said, to the British reader. Ostensibly, Kipling is advising and exhorting the new American candidate for imperialist honours. But the inner message is surely different. The poem manages both to praise those who administer the British Empire in the field, and to express their feeling that their efforts go unrecognized, or insufficiently rewarded. Though it appears to be morally austere (the work is its own reward, however hard) it combines that with an invitation to moral self-congratulation. The reader becomes one of the 'peers' who will eventually pass judgement on the American achievement. The language, apparently open and plain, is actually subtle and devious. The title itself is a brilliant piece of legerdemain, and in that sense, characteristic. It expresses feelings which, as Kipling's reputation indicates, many people felt, for themselves, or for their families (notice the first verse). And like a great deal of 'popular' literature, it leaves such feelings in a confused state.■

4.20   Stead uses two quotations to define the Georgian achievement. The first from a
        review by a conservative critic, Arthur Waugh, the second from a letter of Rupert
        Brooke's:

> 'We write nothing that we might not speak' proclaims the new rebellion in
> effect: 'We draw the thing as we see it for the God of things as they are.
> Every aspect of life shall be the subject of our art, and what we see we shall
> describe in the language we use every day.' (*The New Poetic*, p 82.)

> [My habit of mind] consists in just looking at people and things as
> themselves – neither as useful nor moral nor ugly nor anything else; but
> just as being. (*The New Poetic*, p 82.)

Poetry, in other words, is neither a vehicle for large-scale arguing out of political
or religious opinions, nor is it to be devoted to expressing special kinds of experience
which only poets can grasp. Poetry should express the immediate, the directly-
known, without pre-judgement. Now it can at once be argued that, as a programme,
that leaves a great deal to be said. 'Things as they are', 'things as themselves', can
be, and in Georgian hands often became, a recipe for dullness and triviality. Brooke,
for example, in his poem 'The Great Lover' printed in the 1915 Georgian anthology
(see also his *Collected Poems*, pp 132–5), expressing – not his love affairs – but his
fondness for various ordinary experiences, does so by making a long list of 'things I
have loved.' But he is not always successful in finding words to *convey the experience of
having loved them*, and while this is *partly* a matter of talent, it is also a question of
realizing that successful poetry requires something more than names and assertions.

T. E. Hulme, in an essay written in 1913–14 called 'Romanticism and Classicism',
which deeply influenced the literary criticism of this century, wrote:

> The great aim is accurate, precise and definite description. The first thing
> is to recognise how extraordinarily difficult this is. It is no mere matter of
> carefulness; you have to use language, and language is by its very nature a
> communal thing; that is, it expresses never the exact thing but a compromise
> – that which is common to you, me and everybody. But each man sees a
> little differently, and to get out clearly and exactly what he does see, he
> must have a terrific struggle with language, whether it be with words or the
> technique of other arts. Language has its own special nature, its own
> conventions and communal ideas. It is only by a concentrated effort of the
> mind that you can hold it fixed to your own purpose. (Hulme in
> *Twentieth Century Literary Criticism*, ed. Lodge, p 101.)

There is more to poetry than accurate description, but Hulme states here a funda-
mental truth about language, that no poet can ignore. Language *is* a communal
thing, and to adapt it to individual experience, as any poet tries to, is very hard work.
In this respect, Georgian poets seem not to have thought deeply enough about the
difficulty of their task. Nevertheless, taking the two quotations given by Stead at
their positive value, one can see why a critic like James Reeves claimed that Hardy
and Housman were 'father-figures' to Georgian poetry.

4.21   Reeves mentions another point (it may also have occurred to you): rural or rustic
        subject matter. We will conclude this discussion of Georgian poetry by looking at
        some more poems of a rural type. Read them through, then make notes on the
        questions that follow.

Moonlit Apples

At the top of the house the apples are laid in rows,
And the skylight lets the moonlight in, and those
Apples are deep-sea apples of green. There goes
    A cloud on the moon in the autumn night.

A mouse in the wainscot scratches, and scratches, and then
There is no sound at the top of the house of men
Or mice; and the cloud is blown, and the moon again
    Dapples the apples with deep-sea light.

They are lying in rows there, under the gloomy beams;
On the sagging floor; they gather the silver streams
Out of the moon, those moonlit apples of dreams,
    And quiet is the steep stair under.

In the corridors under there is nothing but sleep.
And stiller than ever on orchard boughs they keep
Tryst with the moon, and deep is the silence, deep
    On moon-washed apples of wonder.

The Waggoner

The old waggon drudges through the miry lane
   By the skulking pond where the pollards frown,
Notched, dumb, surly images of pain;
   On a dulled earth the night droops down.

Wincing to slow and wistful airs
   The leaves on the shrubbed oaks know their hour,
And the unknown wandering spoiler bares
   The thorned black hedge of a mournful shower.

Small bodies fluster in the dead brown wrack
   As the stumbling shaft-horse jingles past,
And the waggoner flicks his whip a crack:
   The odd light flares on shadows vast

Over the lodges and oasts and byres
   Of the darkened farm; the moment hangs wan
As though nature flagged and all desires.
   But in the dim court the ghost is gone

From the hug-secret yew to the penthouse wall,
   And stooping there seems to listen to
The waggoner leading the gray to stall,
   As centuries past itself would do.

Old Man

Old Man, or Lad's-love, – in the name there's nothing
To one that knows not Lad's-love, or Old Man,
The hoar-green feathery herb, almost a tree,
Growing with rosemary and lavender.
Even to one that knows it well, the names
Half decorate, half perplex, the thing it is:
At least, what that is clings not to the names
In spite of time. And yet I like the names.

The herb itself I like not, but for certain
I love it, as some day the child will love it
Who plucks a feather from the door-side bush
Whenever she goes in or out of the house.
Often she waits there, snipping the tips and shrivelling
The shreds at last on to the path, perhaps
Thinking, perhaps of nothing, till she sniffs
Her fingers and runs off. The bush is still
But half as tall as she, though it is as old;
So well she clips it. Not a word she says;
And I can only wonder how much hereafter
She will remember, with that bitter scent,
Of garden rows, and ancient damson trees
Topping a hedge, a bent path to a door,
A low thick bush beside the door, and me
Forbidding her to pick.
                              As for myself,
Where first I met the bitter scent is lost.
I, too, often shrivel the grey shreds,
Sniff them and think and sniff again and try
Once more to think what it is I am remembering,
Always in vain. I cannot like the scent,
Yet I would rather give up others more sweet,
With no meaning, than this bitter one.
I have mislaid the key. I sniff the spray
And think of nothing; I see and I hear nothing;
Yet seem, too, to be listening, lying in wait
For what I should, yet never can, remember:
No garden appears, no path, no hoar-green bush
Of Lad's-love, or Old Man, no child beside,
Neither father nor mother, nor any playmate;
Only an avenue, dark, nameless, without end.

Tell me not here

Tell me not here, it needs not saying,
    What tune the enchantress plays
In aftermaths of soft September
    Or under blanching mays,
For she and I were long acquainted
    And I knew all her ways.

On russet floors, by waters idle,
    The pine lets fall its cone;
The cuckoo shouts all day at nothing
    In leafy dells alone;
And traveller's joy beguiles in autumn
    Hearts that have lost their own.

On acres of the seeded grasses
    The changing burnish heaves;
Or marshalled under moons of harvest
    Stand still all night the sheaves;
Or beeches strip in storms for winter
    And stain the wind with leaves.

Possess, as I possessed a season,
 The countries I resign,
Where over elmy plains the highway
 Would mount the hills and shine,
And full of shade the pillared forest
 Would murmur and be mine.

For nature, heartless, witless nature,
 Will neither care nor know
What stranger's feet may find the meadow
 And trespass there and go,
Nor ask amid the dews of morning
 If they are mine or no.

■ What do you think each poem is about? Are they descriptions, or something else, and if so what? How successful is each poet in conveying thoughts or feelings through his handling of the scene?

Discussion

The main concern of 'Moonlit Apples' is to conjure up an atmosphere, dreamy, magical, lonely, mysterious. I think it does it quite well, but that it conveys no thought or feeling beyond that. It's not description, but evocation: the mood once evoked, there is nothing else to the poem. 'The Waggoner' also seems mainly concerned to conjure an atmosphere of mystery, even of menace: why *is* the ghost listening to the waggoner? But the earlier verses raise other feelings and implications that make it more than mere description. 'Notched dumb surly images of pain' – whose pain? Of the trees that have been pollarded? Or of the poet's implicit feelings about doing this to trees? Why do the oak-leaves 'wince'? And the 'small bodies [that] fluster' in fear of their lives as the cart lumbers past keep up the suggestion of pain, of violent spoliation. A different more complex purpose seems to work in these details, never fully declared or related to the disappointingly conventional ending. It seems to me both a more interesting and a less successful poem than 'Moonlit Apples'.

'Old Man' includes some carefully detailed description – of the child picking the bush, of its smell, of the withered herb. But it is clear from the beginning that the main concern is with the experiences associated with the herb. The first few lines question the appropriateness of its name, raising deep issues of the relation of names to things; the middle section introduces a second person into the poem (the writer's daughter) and looks briefly forward to her adult life; the third section plunges back in time, into the writer's hidden past, and deep into his memories. Perhaps 'non-memories' would be the better term. The physical existence of the herb focuses each of these experiences. The main concern of the poem, then, is to use the herb as a way of talking about troublingly elusive experiences, connected with memory, childhood, growing up etc. 'Tell me not here' has as its main concern the writer's fear and resentment about death. The descriptions of natural scenes express his fondness for life, and his extreme reluctance to give it up. He sees nature as a *femme fatale*, who betrays the poet-lover, and condemns him to lonely death. The tone of the poem attempts an urbane, sophisticated acceptance of his inner pain (as between men of the world accustomed to betrayal by mistresses) and addresses the reader as one whose illusion that things might be different for him needs to be corrected. Both these poems, in contrast with the previous pair, use the natural scene to communicate a central human experience.

The last question asked for your view of each poem's success in conveying thoughts and feelings by means of description. I would say that 'Moonlit Apples' and 'Old Man' were, in their very different ways, entirely successful; and 'The Waggoner' and 'Tell me not here' only in part. 'Moonlit Apples' hardly needs detailed comment, but the complex effects of 'Old Man' are worth exploring. What the poet does here is provide a situation out of which his ideas can *emerge*. The reader shares in the poet's experience of discovering the conclusion by sustained pondering of an actual situation. Notice the hesitant, circling movement of the opening lines, the way that first sentence extends itself in a series of additions, rhythmically marked out by the commas; and the careful back-and-forth piling up of different feelings about 'the names'. The second section is more straightforward, moving away from the poet's thinking into the world of observation, which then becomes the solid basis for the last section where the poet's inner experience is again the subject. When it begins, notice once more the rhythms of the opening lines:

> I – too – often shrivel – the grey threads
> Sniff them – and think – and sniff again – and try
> Once more to think – what it is – I am remembering,
> Always in vain.

Isn't that how it moves? And then as the truth emerges in those extraordinarily powerful closing lines, the rhythm develops emphasis and finality. Notice too how the poem uses the scene it has established to provide a metaphorical complex for the lost memories. It is made up of negatives.

> *No* garden appears, *no* path, *no* hoar-green bush
> Of Lad's-love, or Old Man, *no* child beside,
> *Neither* father *nor* mother, *nor* any playmate

It is a non-scene for a non-memory, vivid language both for the unrecoverable experience, and for the inner bleakness and desolation that – we now see – has everything to do with the poet's inability to recover it. There is nothing to recover, and that, precisely, is the problem. We can say that the poem thinks through the situation that defeated the writer in his life. It expresses the 'nothing', the negation, the vacuity, that as a man, he cannot speak about.

Later in the course, we'll be discussing an idea of T. S. Eliot's called 'the objective correlative' – a somewhat ponderous term by which Eliot meant the poetic structure and method of such a poem as 'Old Man'. It builds up a situation which conveys the poet's feelings to the reader without the poet claiming such feelings in his own person. The poet of 'Old Man' recounts what he sees, and what he thinks about it. He says nothing explicit about his feelings, yet the poem has – I hope you will agree – emotional intensity and power. The herb and the situation built round it, is the 'objective correlative' for these feelings. I mention this now, because it's important in 'modernist' thinking about poetry. Here, a poem with no claims to being 'modernist', nevertheless illustrates that idea.

'Tell me not here' is, to my thinking, less satisfactory in this respect. Nature is an 'enchantress' in the first verse, seducing the writer with her various sources of pleasure, but in the last verse, she is 'witless', an adjective that contradicts the notion of a skilful magician, to say nothing of a clever and attractive woman. The basic situation of the poem breaks down, and bitter feelings previously implied, are now directly asserted. The actual descriptions, too, are less telling than they need to be. 'Aftermaths of soft September', 'marshalled under moons of harvest', – these rely too heavily on *sounding* well. And does 'burnish' with its metallic associations evoke the scene the poet wants? The writing is accomplished, 'stylish', but it seems to me to need the kind of descriptive force of 'Old Man' or (in its different way) 'The Waggoner' to sustain the notion of nature as an enchantress. Another, though probably a more personal reaction, is my feeling that somebody who thinks they 'possess' nature because they are sensitive to beauty, is self-indulgent, theatrical.

Two colleagues reacted differently to 'Tell me not here'. One commented: 'I think you are rather hard on this poem. I don't see it as an expression of "the writer's fear and resentment about death". It seems to me to be an ironical recognition on the part of the poet of nature's invincibility (she will kill him too in time), and of the fact that his love affair with her is so one-sided. By "witless" he means "not aware, not guided by reason", rather than "stupid". He knows very well that "witless nature" takes no notice of him.' Another disliked it more strongly: 'It's difficult to be sure that it's about death. Nobody can miss the "resentment", but where is the "fear"? On the other hand, it's not obviously about anything else. I don't like it. Musically, it is very competent, but the element of self-congratulation is very unattractive. I wonder if it isn't "sexist" in attitude? The enchantress metaphor runs away with him. At the end, he apparently despises nature, turning on her as if she were a mistress who'd cast him off. He calls nature "witless" out of spite. In fact, I don't think this poem altogether knows what it is doing.'∎

4.22   'Moonlit Apples' by John Drinkwater appeared in *Georgian Poetry 1918–1919*; 'The Waggoner' by Edmund Blunden (who contributed several other poems to *Georgian Poetry 1919-1922*) appeared in 1920; 'Old Man' by Edward Thomas appeared in *Last Poems* (1918) and 'Tell me not here' by A. E. Housman appeared in *Last Poems* (1922).

4.23   Ezra Pound described the poetry being written at the turn of the century as follows:

> The common verse of Britain from 1890 to 1910 was a horrible agglomerate
> compost, not minted, most of it not even baked, all legato, a doughy mess
> of thirdhand Keats, Wordsworth, heaven knows what, fourth-hand
> Elizabethan sonority, blunted, half-melted, lumpy. (Stock *Poet in Exile*, p 87.)

Mainly, he had in mind the derivative styles we looked at in Section 3, but a similar judgement came to be applied to later Georgian poetry, and this is the key issue. Was Georgianism a genuine, though limited, break from the habits of the nineteenth century, or was it an updated version of those habits? It all depends on how you define 'Georgianism'. If you stick to Marsh's anthologies, you will find many derivative and vapid poems but overall the evidence seems to me contradictory. Marsh's uncertain judgement defeats any fair summary. What critical principle *could* bring between the same covers the different kinds of poem we looked at from the 1918 anthology? And the same applies to the later volumes – Graves and Sassoon (at his most satirical and angry) appear in 1920, and Graves and Blunden in the last. Not major poetry, perhaps, but certainly not a pale imitation of Wordsworth and Keats. Yet if we look at the weaker poems of Stephens, de la Mare, Drinkwater, and Freeman, the hostile opinion seems justified. My own tentative suggestion is that the Georgian anthologies are too indiscriminate to be assessed as a whole – *except* for that strand of attention to poets expressing a fresh, but undemanding, quality of individual experience – that 'realism' that readers found so invigorating after the suffocating stridencies of the hortatory and argumentative writing of some established Edwardian writers.

But if we move to the work of poets like Edward Thomas, Edmund Blunden and Andrew Young, a more interesting answer emerges. They found a way to make positive use of the Georgian recipe, especially of the Georgian rural poem, whose usual forms became, quite fairly, the butt of later criticism as the perfect literary anodyne. If you want to pursue this, you will find more examples of their work in James Reeves' Penguin anthology, *Georgian Poetry*, and you can decide for yourselves how far they are imitations of a faded tradition, or not. Here is one comment on Blunden, though, that has relevance to the poems of Thomas and Young:

> The method of . . . Blunden's best work [is] a sort of illuminated documentary, or, as he himself has termed it, 'a camera and single epithet', which he regards as the sole instruments proper for the use of a 'plain man', and therefore of an English poet. . . . The basis of the poetic method . . . is never to go far beyond appearances. It is essentially descriptive, and although Blunden has learnt from the Romantics to invest natural objects with feeling, he does not convert them into symbols, or use them as visionary media. When he looks at a grain of sand, he does not see a world in it, but just carefully looks. . . . Throughout the twenties, Blunden did remain a 'Nature poet' . . . this limitation was inherent in his method. His resources were drawn from only a single strand of the English poetic tradition.
> (Bolt *Poetry of the Twenties*, pp 43–5.)

On this notion of Georgianism, then, the movement produced some excellent poetry, but within strict limits.

Against that, though, we can quote James Reeves, for whom the chief Georgian poets are de la Mare, Davies, Blunden (pre-eminently), Thomas and Sassoon, and he defines the characteristics of this group in this way:

> The Georgians can offer virtues which seem to have deserted modern poetry and which might be regained if we want to see poetry once more in its wholeness. These qualities are: natural simplicity, emotional warmth, and moral innocence. . . . Where they are most clearly differentiated from the post-Georgians is in their accessibility to unsophisticated emotion. It is this sophistication, pre-eminent in the early poems of Eliot, which is lacking in the Georgians; lack of sophistication is perhaps the principal barrier between the modern reader and the Georgians. To read any poetry since 1935 which is currently considered significant is to be aware of this sophistication: it reveals itself mainly in a mistrust of direct emotion, of a simple response to primary experience, and of direct passionate utterance. The most characteristic poetry of today expresses anxiety, self-doubt, and self-hate, a sense of knowing too much, fear of being caught with the heart exposed.
> (Reeves *Georgian Poetry*, pp xx-xxi.)

The argument here is perhaps too loaded to stand up to close analysis. 'Unsophisticated emotion' is a good defence of Georgian virtues, but 'anxiety, self-doubt and self-hate' are not any the less 'direct emotion' because they need another kind of expression than that required by 'emotional warmth'; and while there is a kind of 'sophistication' that springs from lack of feeling, another emerges from the conviction that 'feeling' is too complicated an experience to be 'direct' about. Also, it is interesting to find Reeves defending Georgian writing for qualities intensively admired by the 'modernist' W. B. Yeats. 'Direct passionate utterance' found impressive voice in Yeats' poems of the 1930s.

But this is a major issue to come back to, when you have read Eliot, Pound and perhaps Auden. The point of this unit has not been to settle arguments, but to illustrate them, and to introduce you to the kind of poetry that developed out of the Georgian movement. You must decide yourself how it compares with other kinds.

REFERENCES

Poetry

Austin, Alfred (1890) *English Lyrics*, Macmillan.

Asquith, Herbert (1916) *The Volunteer and Other Poems*, Sidgwick & Jackson.

Blunden, Edmund (1930) *Poems 1914–1930*, Cobden Sanderson.

Bridges, Robert (1936) *Poetical Works*, Oxford University Press.

Brooke, Rupert (1918) *Collected Poems*, Sidgwick & Jackson.

Davies, W. H. (1963) *Complete Poems*, edited by Sacherevell Sitwell, Jonathan Cape.

Drinkwater, John (1923) *Collected Poems*, Sidgwick & Jackson.

Eliot, T. S. (1963) *Collected Poems 1909–1962*, Faber. (Set book.)

Eliot, T. S. (1967) *Poems Written in Early Youth*, Faber.

Georgian Poetry 1911–1912, (1912) The Poetry Bookshop.

Georgian Poetry 1913–1915, (1915) The Poetry Bookshop.

Georgian Poetry 1916–1917, (1918) The Poetry Bookshop.

Georgian Poetry 1918–1919, (1920) The Poetry Bookshop.

Georgian Poetry 1920–1922, (1922) The Poetry Bookshop.

Gibson, Wilfred W. (1914) *Thoroughfares*, Elkin Matthews.

Graves, Robert (1916) *Over the Brazier*, The Poetry Bookshop.

Hardy, Thomas (1952) *Collected Poems*, Macmillan.

Poems of Thomas Hardy: A New Selection, (1974) selected with an Introduction and Notes by T. R. M. Creighton, Macmillan. (Set book.)

Housman, A. E. (1922) *Last Poems*, Jonathan Cape.

Housman, A. E. (1939) *Collected Poems*, Jonathan Cape.

The Essential James Joyce, (1963) edited by H. Levin, Penguin.

A Choice of Kipling's Verse Made by T. S. Eliot, (1941) Faber.

The Complete Poems of D. H. Lawrence, (1964) edited by Vivian de Sola Pinto and F. Warren Roberts, Heinemann.

The Complete Poems of Walter de la Mare, (1965) Faber.

Nichols, Robert (1919) *Ardours and Endurances*, Chatto & Windus.

Pound, Ezra (1968) *Collected Shorter Poems*, Faber.

The Translations of Ezra Pound (1970), with an Introduction by Hugh Kenner, Faber.

Sassoon, Siegfried (1957) *Collected Poems 1908–1956*, Faber.

Stephens, James (1965) *Collected Poems*, Macmillan.

Thomas, Edward (1936) *Collected Poems*, Faber.

The Poems of William Watson (1905), Bodley Head.

Williams, W. C. (1951) *Collected Earlier Poems*, McGibbon and Kee.

Yeats, W. B. (1950) *Collected Poems*, Macmillan. (Set book.)

Young, Andrew (1974) *Complete Poems*, Secker & Warburg.

Criticism

Alvarez, A. (1958) *The Shaping Spirit*, Chatto & Windus.

Beal, Antony (ed.) (1955) *D. H. Lawrence: Selected Literary Criticism*, Heinemann.

Bolt, Sidney (1967) *Poetry of the Twenties*, Longman.

Cox, C. B. and Dyson, A. E. (eds.) (1972) *The Twentieth-Century Mind*, Oxford University Press.

Davie, Donald (1973) *Thomas Hardy and British Poetry*, Routledge & Kegan Paul.

Eliot, T. S. (ed.) (1954) *Literary Essays of Ezra Pound*, Faber.

Eliot, T. S. (1957) *On Poetry and Poets*, Faber.

Eliot, T. S. (1963) *Selected Prose*, edited by John Hayward, Penguin.

Kenner, Hugh (1951) *The Poetry of Ezra Pound*, Faber.

Leavis, F. R. (1960) *New Bearings in English Poetry*, Penguin. (Set book.)

Lodge, David (ed.) (1972) *Twentieth-Century Literary Criticism*, Longman.

Martin, Graham and Furbank, P. N. (eds.) (1975) *Twentieth-Century Poetry: Critical Essays and Documents*, The Open University Press (Course Reader).

Murray, J. Middleton (1920), *Aspects of Literature*, Essay Index Reprint Series, Books for Libraries.

Press, John (1969) *A Map of Modern English Verse*, Oxford University Press. (Set book.)

Reeves, James (1962) *Georgian Poetry*, Penguin.

Ross, R. H. (1967), *The Georgian Revolt: Rise and Fall of a Poetic Ideal*, Faber.

Stead, C. K. (1964), *The New Poetic*, Hutchinson University Library. (Set book.)

Stock, Noel (1964), *Poet in Exile*, Manchester University Press.

ACKNOWLEDGEMENTS

Grateful acknowledgement is made for the use of copyright material in this unit:

Herbert Asquith, 'The Volunteer' from *The Volunteer and other Poems*, 1916, Sidgwick & Jackson.

Edmund Blunden, 'Winter: East Anglia' and 'The Waggoner' from *Poems 1914-1930*, Gerald Duckworth & Co.

Robert Bridges, 'A Passer By' from *The Poetical Works of Robert Bridges*, 1936, Oxford University Press.

W. H. Davies, 'The Bird of Paradise' and 'The Kingfisher' from *The Complete Poems of W. H. Davies*, 1963, Jonathan Cape and Wesleyan University Press. Reprinted by permission of Mrs H. M. Davies.

Walter de la Mare, 'Full Moon', 'Miss Loo' and 'Titmouse' from *The Complete poems of Walter de la Mare*, 1969, Faber and Faber. Reprinted by permission of the literary trustees of Walter de la Mare and the Society of Authors.

John Drinkwater, 'Moonlit Apples' from *Collected Poems*, 1923, Sidgwick & Jackson.

T. S. Eliot, 'La Figlia Che Piange' and 'Preludes IV' from *Collected Poems 1909-1962*. Reprinted by permission of Faber and Faber. Also published by Harcourt Brace Jovanovich. Copyright 1936 Harcourt Brace Jovanovich Inc, copyright 1963, 1964 T. S. Eliot. Reprinted by permission of the publisher. T. S. Eliot, 'The Death of Saint Narcissus' from *Poems Written in Early Youth*. Reprinted by permission of Faber and Faber. Also published by Farrar, Straus & Giroux Inc, and reprinted with their permission.

Robert Graves, extract from 'It's a Queer Time' from *Over the Brazier*, 1916. Reprinted by permission of the author.

Thomas Hardy, 'A Countenance' from *Collected Poems*. Reprinted by permission of the Trustees of the Hardy Estate, Macmillan London and Basingstoke, The Macmillan Company of Canada, and Macmillan Publishing Co. Inc, New York. Copyright 1928 Florence E. Hardy and Sydney E. Cockerell, renewed 1956 Lloyds Bank Ltd. Thomas Hardy, 'The Walk' and 'Ah, are you digging on my grave' from

Collected Poems. Reprinted by permission of the Trustees of the Hardy Estate, Macmillan London and Basingstoke, The Macmillan Company of Canada and Macmillan Publishing Co. Inc. New York. Copyright 1925 by Macmillan Publishing Co. Inc.

A. E. Housman, 'Others, I am not the first' and 'Loveliest of trees' from *Collected Poems*. Reprinted by permission of the Society of Authors as the literary representative of the Estate of A. E. Housman and Jonathan Cape Ltd. Also from 'A Shropshire Lad', authorized edition, from *The Collected Poems of A. E. Housman*. Copyright 1939, 1940, © 1965 Holt, Rinehart and Winston Inc. Copyright © 1967, 1968 Robert E. Symons. Reprinted by permission of Holt, Rinehart and Winston, Publishers. A. E. Housman, 'Because I liked you better' from *Collected Poems*. Reprinted by permission of the Society of Authors as the literary representative of the Estate of A. E. Housman and Jonathan Cape Ltd. Also from *The Collected Poems of A. E. Housman*. Copyright 1936 Barclays Bank Ltd. Copyright © 1964 Robert E. Symons. Reprinted by permission of Holt, Rinehart and Winston, Publishers. A. E. Housman, 'Tell me not here, it needs not saying' from *Collected Poems*. Reprinted by permission of the Society of Authors as the literary representative of the Estate of A. E. Housman and Jonathan Cape Ltd. Also from *The Collected Poems of A. E. Housman*. Copyright 1922 Holt, Rinehart and Winston Inc. Copyright 1950 Barclays Bank Ltd. Reprinted by permission of Holt, Rinehart and Winston, Publishers.

James Joyce, 'Tilly' from *Pomes Penyeach*. Reprinted by permission of the Society of Authors as the literary representative of the Estate of James Joyce. Also from *Collected Poems*. Copyright 1927 James Joyce. All rights reserved. Reprinted by permission of The Viking Press Inc. James Joyce, 'I hear an Army Charging upon the Land' from *Chamber Music*. Reprinted by permission of Jonathan Cape Ltd and the Executors of the James Joyce Estate. Also from *Collected Poems*. Copyright 1918 B. W. Huebsch Inc, renewed 1946 Nora Joyce. All rights reserved. Reprinted by permission of The Viking Press Inc.

Rudyard Kipling, 'The White Man's Burden' from *The Five Nations*. Reprinted by permission of Mrs George Bambridge and Macmillan London and Basingstoke. Also from *Rudyard Kipling's Verse*: Definitive edition. Reprinted by permission of Doubleday and Company Inc.

D. H. Lawrence, 'The Humming Bird', 'All Souls' and extract from 'Snap Dragon' from *The Complete Poems of D. H. Lawrence*, Heinemann. Reprinted by permission of Laurence Pollinger Ltd and the Estate of Mrs Frieda Lawrence. Also published by The Viking Press Inc. Copyright © 1964, 1971 by Angelo Ravagli and C. M. Weekley. All rights reserved. Reprinted by permission of The Viking Press Inc.

Robert Nichols, extract from 'The Assault' from *Ardours and Endurances*. Reprinted by permission of Chatto and Windus and the author's literary estate.

Ezra Pound, extract from 'The Plunge', 'The Coming of War', 'The Return' and 'In a Station of the Metro' from *Collected Shorter Poems*. Reprinted by permission of Faber and Faber. Also in *Personae*. Copyright 1926 by Ezra Pound. Reprinted by permission of New Directions Publishing Corporation, New York.

Siegfried Sassoon, 'In the Pink' from *Collected Poems 1908-1956*. Faber and Faber. Reprinted by permission of George Sassoon. Also published by The Viking Press Inc. Copyright 1918 E. P. Dutton Co. All rights reserved. Reprinted by permission of The Viking Press Inc.

James Stephens, 'The Snare' from *Collected Poems*. Reprinted by permission of Mrs Iris Wise, Macmillan London and Basingstoke, The Macmillan Company of Canada and Macmillan Publishing Co Inc, New York. Copyright 1915 Macmillan Publishing Co Inc, renewed 1943 by James Stephens.

Edward Thomas, 'Old Man' and 'October' from *Collected Poems of Edward Thomas*, 1936, Faber and Faber. Reprinted by permission of the author's daughter, Mrs Myfanwy Thomas.

William Watson, 'Song' from *The Poems of William Watson*. Reprinted by permission of George G. Harrap & Co.

William Carlos Williams, 'In Harbour' from *Collected Earlier Poems*, 1957, MacGibbon & Kee. Also published by New Directions Publishing Corporation, copyright 1938 New Directions and reprinted with their permission.

W. B. Yeats, 'All things can tempt me' and 'The Cold Heaven' from *Collected Poems*. Reprinted by permission of M. B. Yeats, Miss Anne Yeats, Macmillan London and Basingstoke, The Macmillan Company of Canada and Macmillan Publishing Co Inc, New York. Copyright 1912 Macmillan Publishing Co Inc, renewed 1940 by Bertha Georgie Yeats. W. B. Yeats, 'Never give all the heart' from *Collected Poems*. Reprinted by permission of M. B. Yeats, Miss Anne Yeats, Macmillan London and Basingstoke, The Macmillan Company of Canada and Macmillan Publishing Co Inc, New York. Copyright 1906 Macmillan Publishing Co Inc, renewed 1934 by W. B. Yeats. W. B. Yeats, 'The Magi' from *Collected Poems*. Reprinted by permission of M. B. Yeats. Miss Anne Yeats, Macmillan London and Basingstoke, The Macmillan Company of Canada and Macmillan Publishing Co Inc, New York. Copyright 1916 Macmillan Publishing Co Inc, renewed 1944 by Bertha Georgie Yeats.

Andrew Young, 'A Prospect of Death' from *Complete Poems* edited by Leonard Clark, Martin Secker & Warburg.

Notes

TWENTIETH-CENTURY POETRY